# Delhi: An Emerging Megacity Region

## Other titles of interest:

Globalisation and Peri-Urban Transformation
Tathagata Chatterji

Habib Rahman: The architect of independent India
Prof. S. M. Akhtar

High-density housing for mixed-income groups
Ranjana Mital and Aneesh Nandi

Smart Urban and Rural Planning Techniques
Harmit Singh Bedi

Fixing Flawed Urban Planning: The Case of Delhi
B.G. Fernandes

Humane Approach to Urban Planning
Priya Choudhary

Geographic Information System for Smart Cities
Prof. TM Vinod Kumar and Associates

Local Area Planning in India
Rishi Dev

Metropolitan Governance: Cases of Ahmedabad and Hyderabad
Dr. Vinita Yadav

India's Urban Confusion: Challenges and Strategies
Edited by Dr. M. Ramachandran

Designing Better Architecture Education: Global Realities and Local Reforms
Dr Manjari Chakraborty

The Ekistics of Animal and Human Conflict
Rishi Dev

Water Conservation Techniques in Traditional Human Settlements
Pietro Laureano

The City Observed: Notes from an Unfolding India
Pallavi Shrivastava

Tirtha at Mukteswar: Understanding its Architecture
Dr. Ranjana Mital and Prabhjot Singh Sugga

# Delhi: An Emerging Megacity Region

P. S. Uttarwar

# COPAL PUBLISHING GROUP

Inspiring for a better future through publishing

Published by Copal Publishing Group
E-143, Lajpat Nagar, Sahibabad,
Distt. Ghaziabad, UP – 201005, India

www.copalpublishing.com

First Published 2017
© Copal Publishing Group, 2017

ISBN: 978-93-83419-38-8 (hard back)
ISBN: 978-93-83419-39-5 (e-book)

Typeset by Bhumi Graphics, New Delhi
Printed and bound by Bhavish Graphics, Chennai

# Preface

I am very glad to have accomplished this task of authoring the book on Delhi, which has been my *karmabhoomi*. It is a reflection of time; each chapter deals with a particular issue or problem of that era. For example, the chapter titled, "Monitoring and Implementation of the Master Plan Policies in Delhi" talks about a fine and meticulous exercise of preparing the Master Plan document. At the same time, implementation of these proposals remains to be an area of concern. From the experience of Delhi, one can say that the Master Plan proposals remain unattended where the role of implementing agencies is not clear, and there is no allocation of resources in terms of land and finance. Non-implementation of some of the Master Plan policies creates an impression that the traditional land use planning has contributed to an unbalanced development of cities, distortion in land and housing markets. Journey of planning continues by adopting and innovating new techniques in the preparation of a Master Plan. During the plan period of MPD-2021, many procedure-based planning approaches for critical areas like unauthorized colonies, etc., were introduced. It was a departure from traditional planning and therefore, there is a chapter titled, "Procedure-based Planning: An Approach for Critical Areas".

It has been a long journey of 35 years which I began in 1981 in Delhi Development Authority. During this time span, I had the opportunity to work on two consecutive Master Plans. I learnt that policies and strategies change, but they maintain the continuity of the overall planning objective. The national capital territory of Delhi is a fast growing megalopolis, and it also contributes to the growth of the National Capital Region (NCR). The urban planning approach has gone through quite some change in India. The chapter, "A Planning Approach for Fast Changing 'Socio-Political' Environment : A Case of Delhi Master Plan" is a testimony to the changes that have taken place in the last two decades in our approach in making a Master Plan.

More importantly, it was here in DDA that the planning and implementation of sub cities like that of Dwarka and Rohini could be seen; designed for a population of one million, where the houses, roads and parks are being built as per sector and layout plans. It's a rare opportunity for a planner to see his work being implemented in such a manner.

This book is organized into three sections. The first section is 'Contemporary Planning' which consists of chapters based on policies and strategies adopted in the Master Plan to deal with current socio-political issues. Over the years, planning policies and procedures have undergone sea changes. The Master Plan document framework remains the same, but at the same time it has become responsive to the changing socio-economic environment. Hence, this section focuses on procedure-based planning, monitoring of planning proposals, etc. It talks about adoption of new planning techniques to meet the challenges posed by ground realities like unauthorized colonies.

The second section deals with planning practices suitable to our conditions. The German concept of environmental planning is very simple and cost effective as far as ground water conservation and protection is concerned. Our cities are going through a terrible water crisis. A German idea of protecting water at the source is adoptable in Indian conditions. Water is also a stabilizing factor as far as cities are concerned. The chapter "Role of Water in Stabilising Cities" explains the current scenario of preparedness of our cities on this front.

The third section discusses planning techniques like Remote Sensing and GIS, available to planners for monitoring and mapping urban sprawl. These are not academic studies or exercises, but practical knowledge acquired during long career in a premier development authority of the country. These planning practices and methods are adoptable in Indian conditions. For example, 'Transit Oriented Development (TOD)' policy has been already put to practice and a green field project at Karkardooma in East Delhi is at implementation stage. Other cities could learn from this experience.

Therefore this work must be viewed as an initial and tentative contribution to what promises to be an important field of study, i.e. urban planning.

Last but not the least; I would like to give special recognition which is due to my family, who provided me with patient understanding and support for all these years. I would especially like to thank my wife Kanchan, my sons Paritosh and Ashutosh, and also my daughter-in-law Sunaina, for their constant encouragement.

New Delhi                                               **P. S. Uttarwar**
May 2016

# Acknowledgement

I am greatly indebted to Prof. (Col.) Prabhakar Misra, former Head of the Department, Human Settlement Analysis Group, Indian Institute of Remote Sensing, Dehradun (India), who initiated me in the field of Remote Sensing and Geographic Information System (GIS). It was his advice and guidance which led to taking up further studies in GIS at ITC, Netherlands. Some of the articles on Remote Sensing & GIS are studies conducted under his guidance at IIRS, Dehradun.

I am thankful to Dr (Prof) D.S. Meshram, President, Institute of Town Planners India for his encouraging attitude, scholarly guidance and invaluable support.

I am also thankful to Ms Paromita (Romi) Roy, co-author of an article on "Transit Oriented Development (TOD) Policy: Case study of East Delhi Hub – Karkardooma TOD project, New Delhi." It's an outcome of her pain staking hard work and research.

I would like to put on record my appreciation to all stakeholders, those who have made significant contribution in my endeavor; it is my great pleasure to thank Mr Rishi Seth from COPAL Publishing who did so much to publish this book.

I am also grateful to my organization Delhi Development Authority, for providing me an opportunity to work and also learn about important fields of study like urban planning, city development and management. I am thankful to my seniors and Vice Chairman DDA for their guidance from time to time.

Last but not the least, I would like to give special recognition which is due to my family, who provided me with patient understanding and support for all these years. I would especially like to thank my wife Kanchan, my sons Paritosh and Ashutosh, and also my daughter-in-law Sunaina, for their constant encouragement.

# Contents

*Preface*                                                                   v

*Acknowledgement*                                                          vii

*Foreword*                                                                 xiii

*Foreword*                                                                 xvii

*About the Author*                                                        xix


**Section 1: Contemporary Planning**

1. **Transit Oriented Development (TOD) Policy:**                            1
   **Case study of East Delhi Hub – Karkardooma**
   **TOD project, New Delhi**

   1.1   Introduction                                                       1

   1.2   Goal of TOD                                                        2

   1.3   Planning and design parameters                                     2

   1.4   Mix of uses                                                        4

   1.5   East Delhi Hub: Karkardooma TOD project                            5

   1.6   Way forward                                                       12

2. **A planning approach for fast-changing**                               15
   **"socio-political" environment: A case of**
   **Delhi Master Plan**

   2.1   Urbanization in India: A challenge                                15

   2.2   Challenges of urban planning                                      16

   2.3   Master plan: Past experience                                      16

   2.4   Flexibility in planning approach                                  19

   2.5   Critical areas that require flexible approach in                  20
         planning

| 2.6 | Master Plan for Delhi 2021 provisions | 20 |
| 2.7 | Bibliography | 22 |

**3. An approach to conservation of built heritage: Delhi master plan provisions** — 23

| 3.1 | Introduction | 23 |
| 3.2 | Delhi's heritage | 24 |
| 3.3 | Conceptual framework on conservation aspect for MPD 2021 | 25 |
| 3.4 | Plan for a conservation zone | 27 |
| 3.5 | Master Plan 2021 proposals | 29 |
| 3.6 | Conclusion | 31 |

**4. Procedure-based planning: An approach for critical areas** — 42

| 4.1 | Introduction | 42 |
| 4.2 | Urban planning: Past experience | 43 |
| 4.3 | New approach: Procedure-based planning | 43 |
| 4.4 | Procedure-based planning for critical areas | 44 |
| 4.5 | Procedure-based planning initiated in MPD 2021 | 45 |
| 4.6 | Procedure for regularization of unauthorized colonies | 45 |
| 4.7 | Conclusions | 50 |

**Section 2: Planning Practices**

**5. Spatial environmental planning: A German concept in urban and environmental planning** — 51

| 5.1 | Introduction | 51 |
| 5.2 | Planning concepts based on environmental consideration | 52 |
| 5.3 | Effectiveness of German planning system | 53 |
| 5.4 | Planning as a "Conflict coordination theatre" | 55 |
| 5.5 | Planning in Germany: Standards versus procedures | 55 |

| | | |
|---|---|---|
| 5.6 | Planning as a "bottom–up process" | 56 |
| 5.7 | Environmental objectives | 56 |
| 5.8 | Water protection zone | 57 |
| 5.9 | Management of river's wholesomeness by co-operative | 58 |
| 5.10 | Planning and implementation of industrial estates | 59 |
| 5.11 | Urban renewal programs | 61 |
| 5.12 | Conclusion | 63 |

**6. Monitoring and implementation of the master plan policies in Delhi** — **64**

| | | |
|---|---|---|
| 6.1 | Introduction | 64 |
| 6.2 | Master Plan for Delhi, 1981–2001 | 64 |
| 6.3 | Monitoring and implementation | 65 |
| 6.4 | Broad lines of the new framework | 69 |
| 6.5 | Conclusions | 71 |

**7. Future trends in urban planning: Changing the tradition of master plan making in the Indian context** — **72**

| | | |
|---|---|---|
| 7.1 | Introduction | 72 |
| 7.2 | Morphology of master plans | 72 |
| 7.3 | Past trends | 75 |
| 7.4 | Limitations of master plans | 76 |
| 7.5 | Emerging trends in urban planning | 76 |
| 7.6 | Conclusion | 78 |

**8. Role of water in stabilizing cities: Case of Delhi city** — **80**

| | | |
|---|---|---|
| 8.1 | Introduction | 80 |
| 8.2 | Existing scenario of water supply in Delhi | 82 |
| 8.3 | Problems of water supply in Delhi | 83 |
| 8.4 | Water management in Delhi | 85 |
| 8.5 | Conclusion | 89 |

**Section 3: Planning Techniques**

**9.  Monitoring and mapping of urban sprawl Delhi, 1988    91**

9.1     Introduction                                         91

9.2     The monitoring                                       92

9.3     Remote sensing and monitoring                        92

9.4     Objectives                                           93

9.5     Material used                                        94

9.6     Instruments used                                     94

9.7     Scope of the study                                   94

9.8     Limitations                                          95

9.9     Study area                                           95

9.10    Delhi: The evolution of the town                     98

9.11    Urbanisation and the growth                         100

9.12    Methodology: Stages of the work                     102

9.13    Land use / land cover classification for urban      103
        area and its environs

9.14    Analysis                                            112

9.15    Conclusions and recommendations                     113

9.16    References                                           114

**10.  Application of GIS and Remote Sensing in            118
      planning, management and monitoring at urban
      fringe areas**

10.1    Introduction                                         118

10.2    GIS and Remote Sensing techniques                    118

10.3    Interpretation of satellite imageries                119

10.4    Change detection                                     120

10.5    Monitoring                                            120

10.6    Detection of vacant land                             122

10.7    Conclusion                                            122

**xii    Index                                              125**

# Foreword

The present book in hand "Delhi: An Emerging Mega City Region" is a compilation of several decades of knowledge and experience gained by Shri P. S. Uttarwar during his tenure as an Additional Commissioner (Planning), Delhi Development Authority. The book comprises of ten chapters mostly related to urban planning of Delhi; it has been grouped in three sections namely: Contemporary Planning, Planning Practices, and Planning Techniques. The first chapter is titled as "Transit Oriented Development (TOD) Policy: Case Study of East Delhi Hub – Karkardooma, TOD Project, New Delhi". In this chapter Shri Uttarwar argues that Transit Oriented Development (TOD) is a planning strategy which integrates the land use and transport system, thereby creating lively, sustainable, pedestrian and cycling-friendly areas in neighborhoods, and encourages people to choose transit over cars for their long commutes. A widely accepted description of TOD is an urban environment with high densities, mixed and diverse land uses, located within easy walkable areas around a transit node. Taking example of 'East Delhi Hub – Karkardooma TOD Project of New Delhi, Shri Uttarwar has demonstrated that TOD policy is the paradigm shift and heralds a new way of linking urban systems to day-to-day living.

The second chapter titled "A Planning Approach for Fast Changing Socio-Political Environment: A Case of Delhi Master Plan" narrates that urban planning in India has gone through considerable changes, and India as an emerging economic power has been pursuing policies towards improving living standards of all the sections of the society. Economic development in terms of per capita income, availability of resources for infrastructure development are the two factors which impacted and shaped policies, approaches and direction of land use planning in the present context. Focus of planning has shifted from 'the principle of controlled development of land' to 'the principle of demand and supply'. Due to this paradigm shift, traditional planning requires to readjust its planning tools like Master Plans and Zonal Plans, taking into consideration ground realities which are acceptable to the masses. The concept of Master Plan and Structure Plan are both being questioned in terms of their nature and effectiveness.

The third chapter in the sequence focuses on an important aspect of conservation of built heritage and mainly focuses on provisions of Delhi Master Plan. In this context, it needs no emphases to mention that Delhi is an ancient city with rich historical heritage, and was a capital for many dynasties and rulers. Each ruler and dynasty left imprints in the form of monuments, heritage buildings and capital complexes. Various Mater Plans of Delhi have made provisions for protection and conservation of build heritage, right from the first Master Plan of Delhi 1962 to the Master Plan of Delhi 2021, and also made conceptual framework and policies for protection and conservation of treasure of built heritage of Delhi.

The chapter "Procedure-Based Planning: An Approach for Critical Areas" underlines that Master Plan in India is the planning instrument which stood test of time and despite criticism, severe limitations and slow pace of implementation have brought certain reforms, flexibility towards achieving goals for urban planning process, with innovative ideas and shift from 'standard-based planning' to 'procedure-based planning'. Current land use planning practice of prescribing uniform standards for all geographic areas irrespective of their socio-economic status or local elements has resulted in incompatible land uses and unauthorized growth, therefore Shri Uttarwar argues that the procedure-based planning integrates local issues like land ownership, socio-economic status and contributes to bottom–up approach to land use planning at zonal and master plan levels.

The chapter titled "Spatial Environmental Planning: A German Concept in Urban and Environmental Planning" brings into focus the German Planning System which has successfully integrated environmental objectives in physical planning, which is yielding high dividends towards sustainable environment. The present drinking water needs of entire Germany are met through ground water and other local resources like river and lakes, thus, saving in massive cost of transportation of water and then treating it. It has also enhanced the quality of water which was released back in rivers and lakes. Shri Uttarwar is of the opinion that German experience has also proved to be cost effective to protect resources at the source than treating them at delivery point.

The aspect of monitoring and implementation of the master plan policies has been reviewed by taking example of Delhi in the chapter "Monitoring and Implementation of Master Plan Policies in Delhi", and it is argued that planning is better than non-planning. A lot of planning projects have been successfully implemented, which have created huge stock of housing as well as large network of infrastructure in the form of drains, water supply lines and roads. It is also contended that during the plan-making stage itself, identification of implementing authorities has led to successful implementation of master plan policies in Delhi.

"Future Trends in Urban Planning: Changing the Tradition of Master Plan Making in the Indian Context" is the chapter which traces the history of master planning process during last the five decades of preparation of

Master Plan by the various state governments and suggest to evaluate the process in terms of their benefits, and draw backs. The chapter also highlights innovative features of Master Plan for Delhi-2021, and recommends to address the issue of governance, policies and process of decision-making more effective.

Water has played an important role in evolution of human civilization and presently half of humanity is living in cities, and within next two decades, nearly 60 per cent of the world's people will be living in cities. The exploding urban population growth creates unprecedented challenges, affecting the sustainability of human urban settlements due to lack of access to safe water and increasing water-related disasters such as floods and droughts. These problems have enormous consequences on the environment, economic growth and development, which need to be addressed in the right earnest, which is highlighted in the chapter titled as "Role of Water in Stabilizing Cities: Case of Delhi City".

Last but not the least, the chapter "Monitoring and Mapping of Urban Sprawl" is also based on the experience of Delhi. The rapid urbanization process and the concentration of population in metropolitan areas is a result of the mass migration of people from rural to urban areas. Over the years, rapid technological advances are also influencing urban growth, and it is out pacing the slow planning process. Large number of slums and squatter colonies are dotting city scene. Shri Uttarwar is of the opinion that the problems are more aggravated by lack of detection mechanism, because urban planners have to depend on information system available for planning, decision making and monitoring so as to detect changes in urban areas, and accordingly update base maps, which forms basis for all planning work. The rapid urban development process has outpaced the traditional techniques of survey, and latest technological innovations like remote sensing techniques would be most appropriate tool to face these challenges.

The experience of master planning of Delhi narrated by Shri P. S. Uttarwar while working in Delhi Development Authority over 34 years, to be exact during 1981–2015, in fact would go a long way in guiding the planners and policy makers to make the present planning system more vibrant, dynamic and transparent.

30th April 2016                             **Prof. Dr. D. S. Meshram**
                          *President, Institute of Town Planners India*
          *Former Chief Town Planner, Town and Country Planning Organisation*
                  *Ministry of Urban Development, Govt. of India*       xv

# Foreword

In this seminal book, the author has critically reflected the challenges and also the opportunities of the (Delhi) Master Plan, one of the oldest and still very relevant spatial planning tools. With his profound practical experience, he has discussed strengths and weaknesses of the past and current Master Plan. Using showcase examples, he has developed new perspectives based on emerging new planning approaches. This is an interesting and fruitful endeavour. Delhi has faced the tremendous problems of city development and infrastructure in times where cities are faster and faster developing into urban mega agglomerations with seemingly unsolvable problems linked to the use of the limited resource of space.

He is not joining the uncritical and superficial public "discussion" which, on the one side, is a self-affirming "Master Plan Bashing", not critically reflecting the function of such a planning instrument and, on the other side, the repetition of the pretty formal insistence that the administrative requirements have to be met rigidly to maintain a top–down order for a spatial structure. Both statements are not really getting the point and are not productively contributing to solve the problems of mega-cities.

The advantage of the reflections compiled in this book is that the discussions of the planning approaches are based on a profound understanding of the processes. Their analysis is giving them an evolutionary perspective. I want to underline only one of the many points: The understanding of planning in India was – and often still is – that a plan is a standard, rather rigidly prescribing what shall be. By analysing the results and the process of the master planning, Author makes a strong point – with illustrating examples – that the planning should develop into a process-based planning. Apart from the clear statement of the necessity of framework planning, he makes it very clear that adjustments are required to make the process more dynamic by a system of bottom–up top–down planning mechanisms.

Many other elucidating examples are put for discussion: Master Plan provisions for build heritage – crucial for saving the historical identification of Delhiites; the Transit Oriented Development Policy – an important policy and development code; Monitoring and implementation of the Master Plan policies – planning is better than non-planning looking at some successes of the Delhi Master Plan; Envisaging Delhi to be a Smart City with world class infrastructure – coping with increasing demands of urbanization; The role of water in stabilising cities – without considering water, any spatial planning is irrelevant; Greenfield development – the new Delhi Master Plan and the example of the sub city and much more. But explore yourself.

June 2015  
Nürnberg, Germany

**Florian Bemmerlein-Lux**  
*Spatial planner and landscape ecologist*

Delhi: An Emerging Megacity Region

# About the Author

P.S. Uttarwar is currently working as Consultant (Planning) in Delhi Development Authority (DDA), after retiring as Additional Commissioner (Planning) DDA, New Delhi, in Sept 2015. He possesses a unique experience of working on second and third Master Plan for Delhi 2001 and 2021, respectively. He was actively involved in micro level planning of Rohini and Dwarka sub-cities, and played an important role in introducing satellite imageries and GIS techniques for planning and mapping purposes.

As the Head of Unified Traffic & Transportation Infrastructure (Planning and Engineering) Centre (UTTIPEC), unit of Delhi Development Authority, he was responsible for finalisation of following policies which were accepted and notified by Government of India.

- Transportation and Transit Oriented Development (TOD) Policy for Delhi Master Plan 2021
- Multimodal Integration (MMI)
- Land Pooling Policy

He pursued his graduation in Architecture from VNIT, Nagpur (India) and postgraduation in Town & Country Planning with specialisation in Urban & Regional Planning, from School of Planning & Architecture, New Delhi (India). In 1989–90, he was awarded a fellowship by the Indo–Dutch programme for post graduation in Land Information System at ITC, Netherlands.

# Transit Oriented Development (TOD) Policy: Case study of East Delhi Hub – Karkardooma TOD project, New Delhi

## 1.1      Introduction

Transit Oriented Development (TOD) is a planning strategy that integrates the land use and transport system, thereby creating lively, sustainable, pedestrian and cycling-friendly areas and neighbourhoods, while encouraging people to choose transit over cars for their long commutes. A widely accepted description of TOD is an urban environment with high densities, mixed and diverse land uses, located within an easy walkable area around a transit node. TOD planning should have two-sided approach:

(i) *TOD retrofitting* – Bringing transit to those locations, where the development already possesses the physical characteristics of that of a typical TOD, i.e. having high densities, but without having transit connectivity at that place.

(ii) *TOD planning* – This approach ensures that necessary planning interventions are made to make urban development more transit oriented by introducing appropriate planning policies and regulations in master plan and land use plan.

TOD is essentially any development, macro or micro, which is focused around a transit node, and facilitates complete ease of access to the transit facility thereby inducing people to prefer to walk and use public transportation over personal modes of transport.

TOD policy shall be a paradigm shift in the way neighbourhoods and city, in general, are planned and heralds a new way of linking urban systems to day-to-day living such that the average person can spend more quality time for social and recreational purposes rather than getting stuck in traffic jams and decreasing one's productivity and health.

As per Master Plan for Delhi 2021, the TOD policy designates a maximum up to 500 meter wide belt (i.e. approximately 5-minute walking distance) on both sides of centre line of the MRTS Corridor as 'TOD Zone', with the exception of areas falling under low density residential areas (LDRA) or formerly called as 'Farm Houses'. TOD zone is a new land use category which allows flexibility in mix of various possible uses, with the exception of polluting and potentially hazardous uses.

## 1.2    Goal of TOD

The goal of the TOD zone is to promote low-carbon high density sustainable development in the city. The policy has the following major aspects:

   (i) Increase in public safety especially for women and children using public transport or walking at night, through changes in key development code aspects such as revised setback norms, dispensing with boundary walls, having built-to-edge buildings with active frontages which provide 'eyes-on-the-street'.

   (ii) Strict planning and regulation of on-street parking to reduce private vehicle use.

   (iii) Approval of projects shall be given through a single-window software-based system to reduce processing time and enable faster-paced (re)development to take place in the city.

   In addition to above, the policy has the following major aspects:

   (a) Delineation of TOD zone on respective zonal development plans (ZDP).

   (b) Preparation of TOD regulations/guidelines for submission and implementation of TOD projects.

   (c) Developing software for single window clearance for approval of layout/building plans.

   (d) Relaying of services as per requirement of re-densification scheme.

## 1.3    Planning and design parameters

The influence zone of MRTS corridors shall be designated as TOD zone where the following development control norms shall apply:

   (a) FAR and density: TOD norms of FAR and density may be availed through the preparation and approval of comprehensive integrated scheme of minimum size 1 Ha.

(b) Maximum ground coverage of 40%. In case of MRTS/government agencies, the minimum plot size for development shall be 3000 sq m.

(c) For Integrated Scheme, a max. FAR of 400

(d) A maximum density of 2000 persons per hectare (PPH).

(e) The entire amalgamated plot will be considered for calculating the FAR and density.

(f) Mandatory EWS FAR of 15% over and above the maximum permissible FAR shall be applicable. Additional FAR may be availed through TDR only, for schemes larger than 1 Ha.

(g) All residents residing in that scheme area shall have to be accommodated within the same scheme

(h) Roads: Of the area taken up for development as integrated scheme, at least 20% of land shall be handed over as constructed roads/ circulation areas to the local body/ road owning agency for public use. However FAR can be availed on the entire amalgamated land parcel.

(i) Green public open space provision: 20% of the area of the amalgamated plot shall be designated as green Public Open Space which shall be designed, developed and maintained by the DE/ agency and will remain un-gated and open for general public at all times, failing which it will be taken over by Public agency.

(j) Social infrastructure: Social infrastructure may be allocated the required built-up area within planned re/development schemes in the form of accommodation reservation, instead of individual plots.

(k) Green buildings: The entire development has to be with minimum 3 star or gold rating as per approved rating agencies and appropriate rebate in the property tax may be applicable.

(l) Impact assessment: Once the Influence Zone plans for TOD areas are prepared by DDA indicating the street networks, indicative amalgamations areas, location of public spaces, active edges, etc. a complete assessment of traffic generation and its dispersal, requirement of services, mitigation measures for environment impact will be done and got approved from bodies concerned so that the redevelopment process through TOD can be effective and beneficial for general public.

## 1.4     Mix of uses

| Land use as per ZDP (At least 50% of total FAR to be as per ZDP use) | Indicative mix of uses within FAR utilization | | | |
|---|---|---|---|---|
| | Minimum Residential* | Minimum Commercial** | Minimum Facilities** | Indicative Mix of Uses within remaining 50% FAR, as per ZDP land use |
| Residential | 30% | 10% | 10% | Of the remaining FAR, at least 20% or more (up to 70% of total) is for residential use. Other uses are permitted up to 30%. |
| Commercial | 30% | 10% | 10% | Of the remaining FAR, at least 40% or more is to be for commercial use. Other uses are permitted up to 10%. |
| Industrial | 30% | 10% | 10% | Remaining 50% of FAR to be for industrial use. |
| Government | 30% | 10% | 10% | Remaining 50% of FAR may be for any government use. |
| Transportation | 30% | 10% | 10% | Remaining 50% of FAR may be for any use after meeting all operational requirements for transportation facilities. Additional norms as per Table 12.7 are applicable. |
| Public and semipublic facilites (PSP) | 30% | 10% | 10% | Of the remaining FAR, at least 40% or more is to be for PSP use. Other uses are permitted up to 10%. |
| Mixed-use | 30% | 10% | 10% | Remaining 50% of FAR may be for any use. |

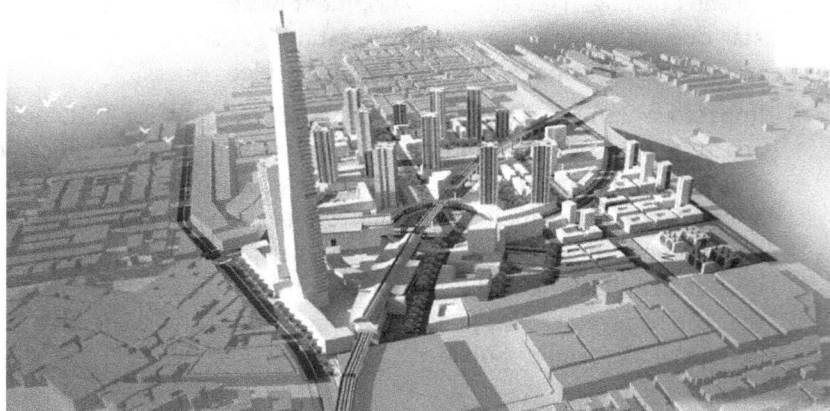

## 1.5    East Delhi Hub: Karkardooma TOD project

### 1.5.1    Background

The proposed site of Karkardooma pilot project falls in the zonal development plan of planning Zone E and the land use of the proposed site is 'residential use'. The Karkardooma smart city hub spread over 74 acres of land would break away from the traditional model of city growth by constructing a pro-pedestrian space where public transport would be encouraged and routine lifestyle needs from recreation to utility would be available within a walking distance of one's home. More than 70% of the site area falls within the 500 m influence zone of two MRTS stations at Karkardooma; therefore, the norms for 'influence zone along MRTS corridors' as per MPD 2021 shall be applicable once the norms are notified. The development control norms and code for TOD as part of the revision of "Transportation (Chapter 12.0) and related sections in Chapter 17.0 (Development Code) and 3.0 (Delhi Urban Area)" has been incorporated.

This TOD project would fulfil the long standing needs of the local community for a hospital, a recreation centre, a school for disabled children, community halls and a large 5-acre community park. The tree-lined park shall be the heart of the community with  a well-demarcated space for use by youngsters for active sports, as well as safe areas for relaxation and exercise for little children and the elderly.

### 1.5.2    Access and connectivity to the site

The site is currently accessible only from the north side through a small stretch on Vikas Marg/ Bhartendu Harish Chandra Marg. On the south side, it is bounded by the railway line and Anand Vihar station, a high tension line, and a proposed 24 m wide zonal plan road. The preliminary traffic impact assessment of the project recommends that a new road having capacity of at least two + two lanes is needed to service the site as the existing junction capacities in the area are not adequate to handle any additional traffic. The proposed new 24 m zonal plan road along the south-east boundary of the site would serve this purpose, besides providing an additional entry/exit to the Anand Vihar railway terminal and helping decongest Vikas Marg.

### 1.5.3    Scenario explored for design option

During the concept phase, numbers of scenarios were explored. Out of many a few were selected to discuss and compare, these are:

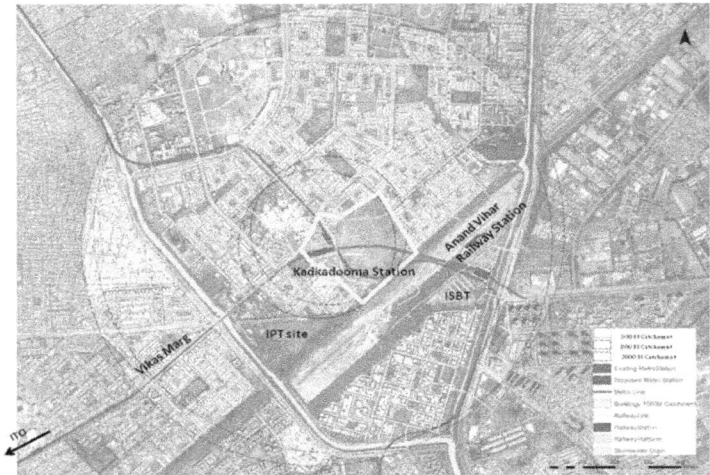

*(A) Business as usual*

Business as usual, i.e. as proposed in MPD 2021

      Residential population = 14060

      Residential = 81.7% of total FAR

      Neighborhood- and community-level facilities = 18% of total FAR

      Usable open space = 15% of land area

      Ground coverage = 15%

      Roads = 15% of land area

      Density = 500 pph

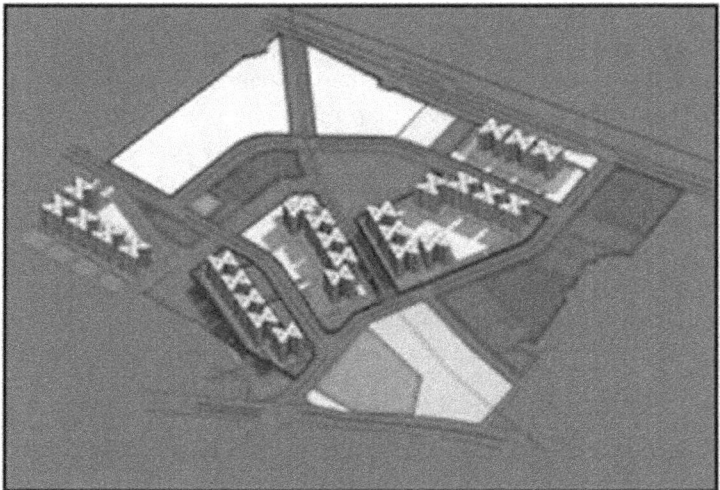

*(B) Design Option 1*

Densification by MPD 2021

    Residential population = 30,375

    Residential = 80% of total FAR

    Neighborhood- and community-level facilities = 20% of total FAR

    Usable open space = 30% of land area

    Ground coverage = 20%

    Roads = 20% of land area

    Density = 1242 pph

*(C) Design Option 2*

Densification by TOD principles

    Residential population = 21,000

    Residential = 50% of total FAR

    Neighborhood-, community- and district-level facilities = 25% of total FAR

    Additional commercial = 25% of total FAR

    Usable open space = 20% of land area

    Ground coverage = 35%

    Roads = 20% of land area

    Density = 830 pph

    Design option 2 found more acceptable.

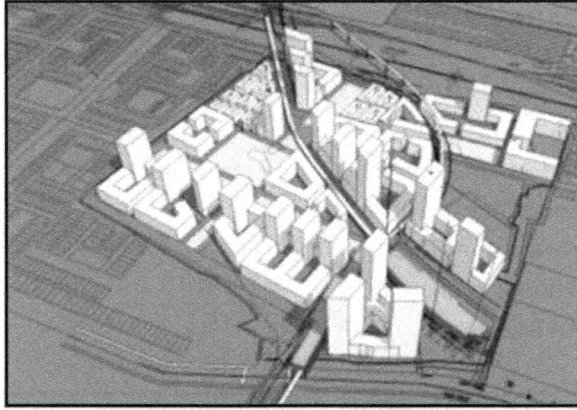

### 1.5.4 Stakeholder consultation process

Stakeholder consultations were conducted – for prioritizing of civic amenities

- RWAs and discussions with residents (formal and informal neighborhoods)
- Trader associations
- NGOs and civil society institutions
- Schools – Workshop with private school children/ discussion with government teachers
- *Pradhans* and local ward counselors

### 1.5.5 Characteristics of planned colonies in surrounding areas

- Mixed-use at main street level (banks, property dealers)
- Re-densifying into G+4 developer flats (with stilts)
- Gated colonies with no thoroughfare
- Rental: Ownership Rate = 30:70
- Typologies: 100–300 sq m
- Costs of home: Rs 2.2 crore+
- Rental costs: Rs 25,000+
- Staff: Drivers, maids, gardeners, guards, vegetable sellers live in informal settlements in both ownership and rent
- RWA concerns: Congestion

- MCD site engineer concerns: Maintenance and infrastructure repair issues

## 1.5.6 Characteristics of informal colonies in surrounding areas

- *Urban villages:* Karkardooma village
- *Un-authorized colonies:*
- *Slums:* Anand Vihar JJ Slum
  1. Mixed-use areas
  2. Rental: Ownership rate = 70: 30
  3. Rental costs: Rs 500–700 per person
  4. Typologies: 16–40 sq m
  5. Issues: Water quality, under-employment, no open spaces for activity; underutilized areas

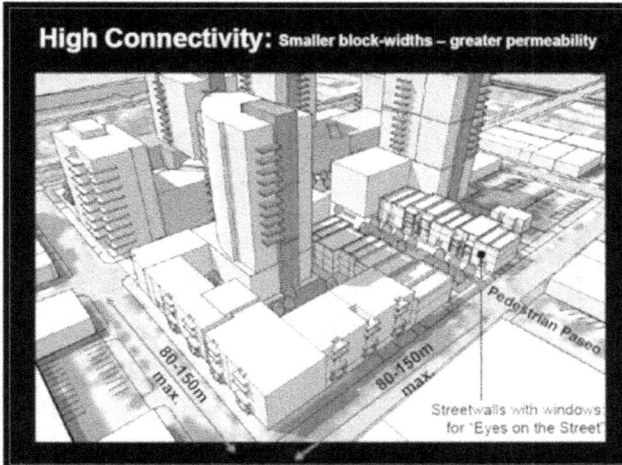

## 1.5.7 TOD concept adopted in pilot project

*Primary design principles*

  (i) Smaller block sizes for greater connectivity
  (ii) Safety through mixed use and eyes on street
  (iii) Minimum 2-hour winter sun access to homes
  (iv) Boundary wall elimination setback reduction/ elimination
  (v) Minimised setbacks and front entries opening on the street

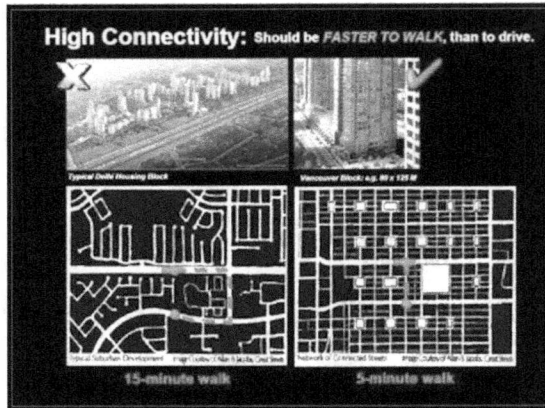

*For commercial/mixed use street*

    (i)   Streets designed with ZERO setbacks

   (ii)   Parking design

  (iii)   Solar access: Minimum 2-hour direct solar access to all living areas.

  (iv)   Ground coverage: Set high minimums

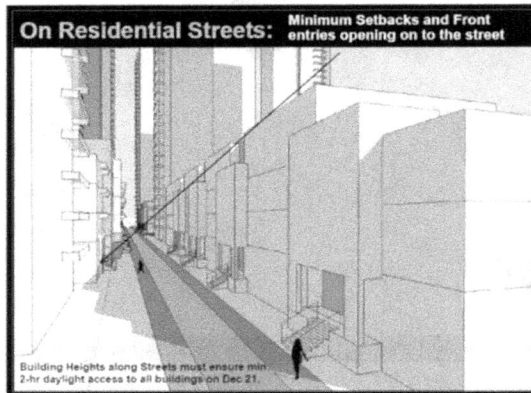

*Primary urban design guidelines*

    (i)   Maximum block length: 150 m

   (ii)   Building height: Distance between buildings = 1.2: 1 (Min)

  (iii)   For residential streets:

  (iv)   Maximum setbacks = 2 m

   (v)   Minimum setbacks = 0 m

  (vi)   For commercial/ mixed-use streets – setbacks = 0

Neighborhood Layout based on Solar Access to homes in Winter.
Minimum standard = 2 hours of sun on longest Winter day (Dec 21).

## 1.5.8    Proposed layout plan

## 1.5.9    Giving everyone a home

Currently, most conversations of housing delivery tend to focus on ownership housing for the high-income bracket (above 60,000 income per month) or the severely low-income bracket (below 10,000 per month). Little focus is given on planning and designing housing typologies for the large majority (>70%) of middle-income population of the city which resides in the unauthorized colonies and slums, and struggles for basic amenities, security and quality of life. TOD aims to accommodate needs of this segment in the housing provision in the city.

Through increased FAR and density, TOD norms may provide a variety of housing types for a range of income brackets and demographic types in the city. This *demographic segment is also most likely to use the MRTS system to work and walk/cycle for daily needs,* given the opportunity to a better quality of life.

To facilitate this, in all TOD integrated schemes, a minimum of 30% of overall FAR shall be mandatory for residential use. Additionally, this mandatory residential component shall comprise of 50% units of size ranging between 32 and 40 sq m (1 BHK) and the balance 50% comprising of homes ≤65 sq m (1–2 BHK). EWS FAR of 15% over and above the permissible FAR will be applicable.

A minimum 10% of FAR for commercial use and minimum 10% of FAR for community facilities is also mandatory. This component shall include the requirements of the residential population in that land parcel and also serve the people visiting/ passing through the area. Mix of uses and FAR utilization for the remaining 50% FAR shall be as per the land use category designated in the zonal plan.

## 1.5.10    Water and services

TOD development will also see a paradigm shift in the provision of water and sewer infrastructure by making the recycling and reuse of water more feasible and efficient, and reducing both – the overall potable water demand, as well as piping/infrastructure costs. The aim would be to efficiently utilize existing water supply without putting external pressure and accommodating more people to benefit from such strategies.

## 1.6    Way forward

High power committee set up by Ministry of Urban Development to suggest how to decongest Delhi has recommended following:

1. Demarcation of influence zone in zonal plans of Delhi needs to be initiated as per MPD 2021 so that ambiguities can be avoided. There could be a fully automated self-evaluation system for any site/scheme area, to be self-tested by potential applicants based on the eligibility criteria provided in the MPD 2021, so that red-tapism and timelines for development can be shortened.

2.  Easy-to-use guidelines and design handbooks should be developed so that general public can understand the interpretation of the policy easily, and designers/developers/ builders can come up with designs/developments that are compliant with the policy's vision and intent.
3.  Parking management district plans need to be prepared and implemented in phases, as TOD schemes roll out gradually in the city.
4.  In order to facilitate "ease of doing business" and fast-paced (re) development, a computerized single window clearance system must be adopted for approval of all TOD projects, the details of which should be included in the regulations for operationalization of TOD policy which needs be notified by DDA.

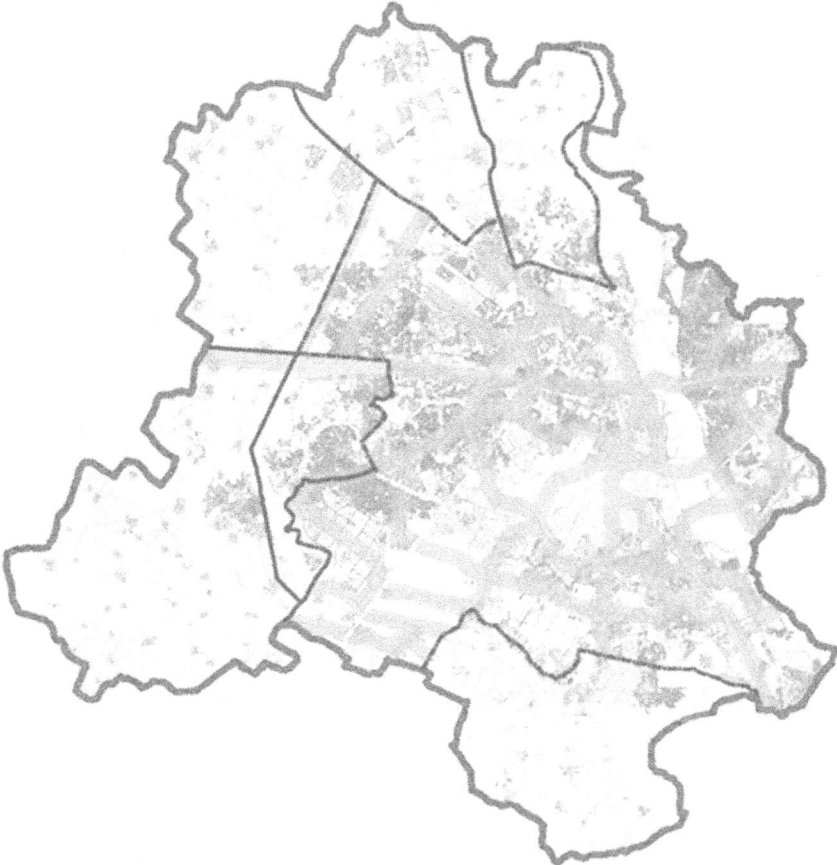

5.  Decentralized infrastructure systems including water recycling and reuse, use of working landscapes and energy demand reduction strategies should be made mandatory in all TOD developments. Further aspects such as co-generation, solar, decentralized STPs, etc., should be highly incentivized.

6.  Process of preparation of the influence zone plans (IZP) or integrated schemes along MRTS corridors based on TOD norms should be initiated by the Delhi Development Authority. All aspects regarding electricity, water, sewer, roads, transportation, utilities, pollution, green areas, etc., and disposal or reuse of debris, etc., should be suitably dealt with by involving concerned agencies/ local bodies, during the preparation of the IZP.

7.  Urban design and connectivity aspects are the key to success of TOD. Therefore, the Authority should prepare/approve integrated TOD schemes and/or influence zone plans, indicating the ROW's, public spaces, build-to lines and connectivity links to Metro stations and probable areas where amalgamation can take place with land parcels of 1 Ha or more. The guidelines for creating arcades, boulevards, paseos, woonerfs and other active streets shall be tentatively indicated in the influence zone plans prepared/ approved by the Authority so that even if development takes place gradually over time, the overall scheme and intent of the TOD-redevelopment process is met over time.

8.  Preparation of the comprehensive and integrated land use and transport system with action plan and strategies for development of an integrated transport system and infrastructure of the city should be taken up on priority basis by the GNCTD and DDA.

# 2

# A planning approach for fast-changing "socio-political" environment: A case of Delhi Master Plan

## 2.1    Urbanization in India: A challenge

Urbanization in India is a challenge, as well as an opportunity; a challenge because of its rapid growth rate, which generally outpaces growth of infrastructure; an opportunity, as it offers better economic avenues. The urban population of India is growing at a faster rate than the growth rate of total population of India. Following are some of the salient features:

(a)  As per census of India 2011, India's population stand at 1.21 billion – 17.5 per cent of world population, and next to China which accounts for 19.4 per cent of the global population.

(b)  Over the last 10 years (2001–11) India has added 181 million population.

(c)  Population of India is almost equal to the combined population of the United States, Indonesia, Brazil, Pakistan, Bangladesh and Japan put together.

(d)  But growth rate has slowed down from 21.15 per cent tin 2001 to 17.64 per cent in 2011.

(e)  For the first time since independence, the absolute increase in population is more in urban areas than in rural areas. Rural population in India stood at 68.24 per cent and urban population 31.16 per cent in 2011.

(f)  Level of urbanization increased from 27.81 per cent in 2001 census to 31.16 per cent in 2011 census.

(g)  The proportion of rural population declined from 72.19 per cent in 2001 to 68.84 per cent in 2011.

(h)  In case of National Capital Territory of Delhi, total population is 16.75 million with composition of 97.5 per cent urban population and 2.5 per cent of rural population in 2011.

(i)  Delhi recorded the decadal growth rate of 21.6% (2001–11).

## 2.2    Challenges of urban planning

Urban planning in India has gone through considerable changes. India as an emerging economic power has been pursuing planning policies with an objective to uplift standard of living of all strata of the society. Economic development in terms of per capita income and availability of resources for infrastructure development, these two factors have impacted and shaped policies, approaches and direction of land use planning in the present context. Focus of planning shifted from 'the principle of controlled development of land' to 'the principle of demand and supply' of open economy. Due to this paradigm shift, traditional planning requires to readjust its planning tools like master plan and zonal plans, in such a way that it recognizes ground realities and it is also acceptable to the people. The concept of master plan and structure plan are both being questioned in terms of their nature and effectiveness. Nevertheless, stakes related to controlling the urban development are crucial for the future of humanity. City dwellers are expected to account for roughly half the world's population in the 21st century. The increase in urbanization of the world population is inescapable and irreversible. Thus, urban planning becomes essential and fundamental for any future development policies.

Over the years, physical and economic development maintained the same pace. However, the process of economic evolution initiated in 1990 has increased the pace of economic development and raised per capita income. Unfortunately, the physical development or planning process could not measure the pace of economic development. This situation led to distortion in the fabric of physical development within and outside the city. An exegesis of planning policies and strategies implemented through master plan document is needed on the basis of past experience of last five decades.

## 2.3    Master plan: Past experience

After the independence of the country in 1947 and to manage post-partition influx of population in the capital city, Delhi Development Authority was set up by the central government. First master plan for Delhi was prepared with help of Ford Foundation, with the perspective up to the year 1981. It adopted a policy of large-scale land acquisition, development and disposal by the government with strict land use zoning (Figure 2.1).

Master plan for Delhi has remained a pioneering document in the field of urban planning in India. With vast experience of plan preparation and implementation, the Delhi Development Authority published second master plan for Delhi in 1991 (MPD 2001) with perspective up to year 2001 (Figure 2.2).

Total area of National Capital Territory of Delhi (NCTD) is 1483 sq km, and total population is 16.75 million with 97.5 per cent population living in urban areas. The decadal growth rate is 21.6% (2001–11).

# Master plan for Delhi – 1962

- The first step towards modern planning in India for integrated development of Delhi.

- Formulated as per the provisions of Delhi Development Act, 1957.

- Promulgated on 1st September, 1962.

- Large scale land aquistion, development and disposal policy.

D.D.A.                                    MPD-2021

**Figure 2.1** Land use plan of master plan for Delhi 1962 (1961–81)
[*Source:* Master plan for Delhi 1962 by Delhi Development Authority]

# Master plan for Delhi – 2001
**MPD – 2001 Promulgated on 1st August, 1990.**
**Projected population – 128 Lakh.**

- Urbanization of further 18000–24000 HA. To accommodate additional population.
- Effective development of NCR to contain rapid population growth.
- The holding capacity increased through the process of law rise high density development.
- Selective densification of urban areas except Lutyens bungalow zone.
- The inner city (walled city & ITS extension and Karol Bag)
- Mass transport system to be multi modal.

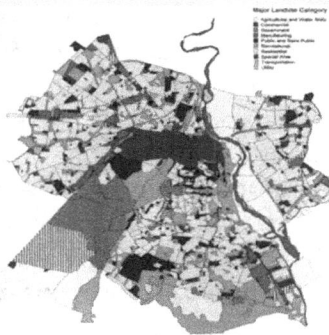

D.D.A.                                    MPD-2021

**Figure 2.2** Land use plan master plan Delhi 2001 (1981–2001)
[*Source:* Master plan for Delhi 2001 by Delhi Development Authority]

A broad review of various planning proposals and processes set during a period of 20 years of master plan for Delhi 2001 indicates that implementation of the proposals remains one of the most difficult tasks due to uncertainties of changing environment. It has been observed that the master plan proposals are successfully implemented where implementing agencies are clearly identified or implementing agencies are local bodies and where master plan for Delhi 2001 (MPD 2001) proposals has become the part of annual action plan or budget of that agency. In most of the cases land was made available to these agencies by DDA. For example, land was allotted for hospitals, schools, fire station, police stations and sewage treatment plants and water treatment plants, etc. Master plan proposals remained unaddressed where:

- Role of agencies was not clear;
- There was no allocation of resources in terms of land or finances, for example: proposals related to the Walled City, Special Area, etc. and
- Traditional areas, non-conforming uses and informal settlements where spatial standards prescribed by master plan were not practical and implementable.

There were also other issues of central importance like urban population and employment growth, land use permissibility, land use intensity, informal sector and incompatible uses which overwhelmed the master plan in the process of its implementation.

Strict land use zoning and policy of compulsory large-scale land acquisition resulted in emergence of large number of unauthorized colonies. Non-access to affordable housing of public sector to majority of population led to growth of these illegal housing settlements popularly known as unauthorized colonies. During the plan period of first master plan and second master plan, around 2300 such colonies came into existence out of which 612 were regularized despite of the fact that these colonies were not fitting into framework of any master plan. Currently, 1639 unauthorized colonies are being considered by the government for regularization. These colonies provide 0.64 million dwelling units (approx. 22% of total) spread over about 9000 hectare of land. Master plan for Delhi 2021 (MPD 2021) has recognized this problem in the following words:

"Unauthorized colonies in Delhi pose a serious human problem as a huge population is living in these colonies. The issue of existing unauthorized colonies has engaged attention since the mid-seventies when a policy for regularization was formulated. 567 out of 607 listed unauthorized colonies were regularized till October 1993, but many more unauthorized colonies have come up since then. Such colonies are to be identified by the Govt. of NCTD. The present method of regularization of unauthorized colonies is by the provision of basic infrastructure to improve the environment. However, regularization has not really brought in any tangible improvement. Effectively, the process has only led to de-facto tenure rights on the land and access to services".

Once these colonies come into existence, they form a vocal political pressure group. In a democratic setup like India where there are three-tier system of elected representatives: municipal representatives, state legislative, assembly representatives and Central Parliament representatives, these unauthorized colonies constitute major part of vote bank. At times it is political compulsion and matter of political survival to regularize these unauthorized colonies even if they do not fit into overall framework of master plan. As a middle path, "procedure-based planning" within the overall framework of master plan is a useful planning tool.

## 2.4 Flexibility in planning approach

Demand in contemporary planning is dynamism, quick adjustment with market forces and approaches to transform policies into land use models. Master Plan document as a planning instrument is very rigid and remains static for perspective period i.e. 20 years in case of Delhi. Basic question is how to make Master Plan document responsive to changing socio-political environment? Bringing flexibility through policies and procedure is one of the ways. Current planning practice heavily depends on rigid space standards or norms to ensure minimum quality of life for planned areas. Such a practice some time results in exclusion of sub-standard areas from planning point of view or areas/clusters which have come up spontaneously. Such a situation is not acceptable to politicians in democratic set up like India.

In order to make planning "inclusive" and not "exclusive", planners started thinking about bringing reforms, flexibility and set implementable goals for urban planning process. Clearly there was preference to adopt in built procedures within a Master Plan document than prescribing standards. So the Master Plan may only state a policy statement for areas which do not fit into planning standards, or areas that are not compatible in terms of land uses & resulted in unauthorized/unplanned growth. On the basis of Master Plan policies, a procedure may be evolved to integrate local issues like land ownership, socio-economic status, etc. It will initiate a bottom–up approach to land use planning in a contrast to entirely top–down approach of Master Plan/ Zonal Plan within current land use planning practice. Such procedure-based planning may help to integrate local issues in the Zonal and Master Plan framework for improving the quality of planning and resource management.

## 2.5 Critical areas that require flexible approach in planning

Over the years, planners are preparing Master Plans and Zonal Plans for perspective of next 20 years. At time it is difficult to anticipate well in advance changes likely to happen in next 20 years or unforeseen circumstances.

So, long-term policies remain unchanged, whereas flexible procedures keep on changing to adjust to the ground realities.

Following areas can be listed where flexibility procedures are advisable to suit to local conditions –

i. Land policies

ii. Public–private partnership (PPP) for land and infrastructure development

iii. Redevelopment of sub-standard areas

iv. Micro level planning

Many more areas can be identified depending on local issues and political requirements.

## 2.6 Master Plan for Delhi 2021 provisions

Master Plan for Delhi 2021 has following provisions which demonstrate flexibility in planning approach and adoptability to local conditions –

a. Local Area Plan – As per the provisions of the law, micro level planning can be taken up to suit to local conditions and characters.

b. Unauthorised colonies – These are the residential areas or clusters which do not fit into parameters of Master Plan in terms of land use and space standards. At the same time these areas are politically sensitive due to large local vote banks. So the government declares procedures/regulations from time to time to provide basic amenities and land rights to inhabitants of these unauthorized colonies within the overall frame work of Master Plan.

c. Villages, special areas and use premises – Within the overall policies of the Master Plan, areas that have grown organically or old areas require special attention. Basic idea is to provide better quality of life and infrastructure by introducing mix land use norms, reasonable parking standards and laying of services.

Procedure-based planning has been initiated in the Master Plan for Delhi 2021, for above-mentioned areas. These aspects and various procedures adopted in the Master Plan for Delhi have been discussed in Chapter 4.0.

**Figure 2.3** Land use plan of urban agglomerations of Delhi and Central National Capital Region [*Source:* Mosaic of land use plans as available on websites (not to scale). Color codes for land use are not uniform]

## 2.7    Bibliography

Delhi Development Authority (2007). Master Plan for Delhi 2021, notified in Gazette of India by the Ministry of Urban Development, Government of India, New Delhi.

Delhi Development Authority (1981). Master Plan for Delhi 2001, notified in Gazette of India by the Ministry of Urban Development, Government of India, New Delhi.

Delhi Development Authority (1957). Master Plan for Delhi 1962, notified in Gazette of India by the Ministry of Urban Development, Government of India, New Delhi.

Gandhi Sagar S. (2007). "Large scale Urban Development in India – Past and Present", Collaboratory for Research on Global project, Stanford University, Working Paper No. – 35 (November).

Government of India (2011). Census of India, New Delhi.

ISOCARP (2000). "Millennium report findings for the future", The work of the congress of ISOCARP 1965-1999, ISOCARP, The Hague, Netherlands.

Uttarwar P. S. (2010). "Procedure based Planning – An approach for Critical areas", Institute of Town Planners India, Volume 7, Number 2 (April–June), New Delhi.

Uttarwar P. S. (2005). "Future trends in Urban Planning: Changing the tradition of Master Plan making in the Indian context", Institute of Town Planners India, Volume 2, Number 3 (July–September), New Delhi.

# 3

# An approach to conservation of built heritage: Delhi master plan provisions

## 3.1    Introduction

Delhi is an ancient city with rich historical milestones and heritage. Historically, Delhi has been a capital city for many dynasties and rulers. Each ruler and dynasty left its impression and footprints in the form of monuments, heritage buildings and capital complexes. The rulers have been conscious of Delhi's past. Their desire to protect the past has influenced protection and conservation of built heritage. Archaeological survey and Public Works Department of British India began this task in the later 19th century, and after independence ASI has become protector of India's heritage. At a later date Master Plan documents attempted to make provisions for protection and conservation of built heritage. Right from the first Master Plan of Delhi 1962 to the Master Plan of Delhi 2021, each document contributed and perfected conceptual framework, approach and policies for protection and conservation of monuments in Delhi.

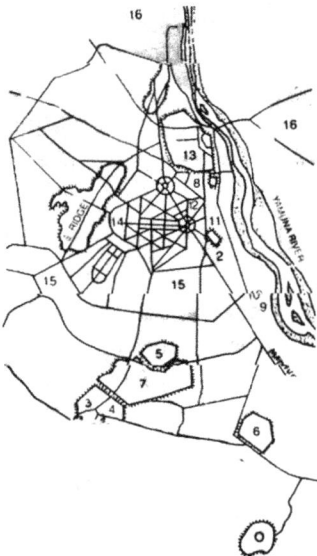

## CITIES OF DELHI

| 1. | PREHISTORIC | |
|----|-------------|--|
| 2. | INDRAPRASTHA | 1450 BC |
| 3. | DILLI AND LALKOT | 100 BC TO 1024 AD |
| 4. | MEHRAULI | 1170 AD |
| 5. | SIRI | 1302 AD |
| 6. | TUGHLAKABAD | 1320 AD |
| 7. | JAHANPANAH | 1344 AD |
| 8. | FEROZABAD | 1351 AD |
| 9. | KHIZRABAD | 1415 AD |
| 10. | MUBARAKABAD | 1433 AD |
| 11. | DINAPANAH | 1530 AD |
| 12. | SHER GARH | 1542 AD |
| 13. | SHAHJAHANABAD | 1648 AD |
| 14. | NEW DELHI | 1911 AD |
| 15. | POST INDEPENDENCE EXPANSION | 1947 AD |
| 16. | POST MASTER PLAN | 1962 AD |

## 3.2     Delhi's heritage

Delhi is an ancient city whose history dates back to the time of Ashoka. This region is uniquely situated in terms of its location. It is a triangular area bound by Yamuna on east side, and by the Aravalis on the south and west side.

For the most part of its history it has been a capital city. The history of Delhi begins from the Ashokan rock edict and comes through centuries to Lutyens' Imperial capital and finally to being the capital of the Indian Republic. Delhi has witnessed numerous ups and downs during this history.

Protecting this heritage represented by a mosaic of capitals and villages is a very big challenge. Through the years right from perhaps Ferozshah's time, rulers have been conscious of Delhi's past, their attitudes and the thinking about past which has influenced protection and conservation of built heritage. Alexander Cunningham's Archaeological Survey and the public work departments of British India were responsible for protection and maintenance of monuments. After independence, ASI has become sole agency for protection of heritage. Even today it continues to function with the same rules and regulations drafted during colonial times. Following is a brief summary of the agencies involved in conservation and provisions of the previous Master Plans.

(1) *ASI*: The rules and legislations for protection of heritage laid down by the British have not changed much till date. Their definition of built heritage is monument based.

(2) *Master Plan for Delhi 1962*: The first master plan was prepared during a time when the concepts of heritage and conservation in India were in their infancy stage. The master plan provided for a number of green spaces to be reserved for the city. Most of these greens were around monuments and this has resulted in protection of a number of monuments.

(3) *Master Plan for Delhi 2001*: In the second master plan the aspect of conservation is dealt under a different subhead. Environment is a section that talks about the conservation of the walled city. The section on special areas also mentions restoring the glory of the Walled City. Urban villages, which are an important component of the heritage, are under the section of Shelter; it rightly mentions that heritage development should be a part of the overall development. The master plan was in accordance with the conservation thought of the day. Due to scattered scheme of conservation thoughts, implementation was a difficult task.

In the 90s, MCD and NDMC published lists of buildings, which were 'protected'. In absence of any legislation or procedures, these monuments remained protected theoretically only.

The ASI protects 164 odd heritage structures in Delhi; besides these, the local bodies have also published the following list:

MCD: 775 buildings

NDMC: 112 buildings

These are ridden with number of problems.

- The world over thinking about heritage has changed radically. The 'Monument' approach has been discarded as being insufficient to protect the built heritage. This built heritage needs to be treated as heritage areas or zones.
- It is necessary to identify what is to be done with these buildings? Who will do it and what conceptual approach lies behind the whole process?
- The lack of appropriate plotting and mapping has resulted in encroachments and deterioration in heritage areas/buildings.

INTACH inventory of Delhi of built heritage of 1208 buildings was published in the year 2000.

## 3.3 Conceptual framework on conservation aspect for MPD 2021

Our heritage is the result of interaction of three forces: (i) *People* occupy a geographical area (ii) *place* where building activity takes place and through (iii) *time* buildings and cities take shape. Understanding of People, Place and Time gives us the context for understanding heritage. It also helps us in evaluating the heritage. Fundamental to the approach for conservation of the built heritage is the understanding of heritage as a Resource. Such an understanding means that like all natural resources, built heritage is also subject to development pressures and exploitation and has to be protected from these threats. The notion of sustainability widely used for natural resources is also applicable for built heritage. Sustainability necessarily means the use of the resources in a matter that does not compromise on the ability of future generations to use and enjoy it.

Managing the natural and built heritage of this complex cultural entity is an enormous task. This cultural entity or *culture region* has a range of *natural* and *built heritage*. This heritage is a valuable resource but is threatened due to pressures of urbanization and development. Historically there had been a symbiotic relationship between the natural and the manmade heritage.

This relationship can be identified as cultural landscapes. Tughlaqabad, the capital of the Tughlaqs, utilized the landform for construction of the capital. Even if the natural and built heritage is within this culture region, there is a whole range of components that have to be identified and conserved. Some of these components are as follows:

- *The river ridge*: Northern, Central and Southern
- *Streams*
- *Agricultural areas*
- *Water bodies*: Ponds, tanks and lakes, Quarried lakes
- *Villages*: Chirag Delhi, Nizamuddin, Kotla Mubarak etc.
- *Historic capitals*: Tughlaqabad, Jahanpahah, Shahjahanabad etc.

Conservation is not freezing a place in time or denying development. Rather it stresses that the development has to occur in relation to the existing built heritage and the relationship with the natural resources. Conservation of built heritage cannot be compartmentalized under a heading and done with. Effective protection and management of built heritage requires that the concerns of heritage be reflected in all areas and be integrated with planning process.

The aim therefore is to formulate a Conservation Management Plan for Delhi's heritage, based on understanding of heritage as a resource.

- *Definition of heritage zones*: The definition of the zones has to be based on understanding of the wholeness of the particular resources. New Delhi is one entity and has to be defined as such. The walled city of Shahjahanabad is again another entity.

## 3.3.1 General policies

Policies to be applied in conservation areas of Delhi have to based on the database of built heritage resources of Delhi. However, a broad generalization may be done based on an accepted attitude towards heritage.

- *Information management*: A detailed database is very important for informed decision-making. The database has to be comprehensive and open ended. It has to be compiled from detailed inventories. The database has to be organized so that it can be answer to multiple criteria queries and is updateable. The decisions for resources management can only come from a thorough database.
- *Legal*: Certain terms, processes, powers, responsibilities duties, etc., regarding conservation should be defined and included in the Act/ Master Plan. Once it is defined in the Act, the process becomes mandatory and ensures that conservation of cultural heritage remains a priority.

- *Administrative:* In administrative setup, the role of any special body should be strictly advisory in nature. There might be a tendency to leave the heritage entirely to this body while the planning process continues regardless.

- *Financial:* The financial policies are to be based on the understanding of ownership status of the structure to be protected. For the private properties various instruments like soft loans, tax relief and tax concessions have to be worked out.

- *Technical:* Structural conservation is a very technical subject and there is a serious lack of data on construction processes and materials. Regular maintenance and the awareness of the occupants are very crucial for the health of the building. At building level, following need to be prepared.
  - Specifications for conservation work
  - Manuals on structures and materials
  - Manuals for housekeeping and maintenance
  - Architectural control guidelines for new development

- *Education and awareness:* Heritage is a vast source of learning and education. Awareness about heritage is very crucial for conservation. All possible means should be used for this purpose. The results of the collected database can be synthesized to feed into the awareness programs.

- *Monitoring and reviewing:* Monitoring and reviewing are very important if the Master Plan provisions are to be implemented. Preparing action plan with prioritization and setting of long- and short-term objectives is a very important task.

## 3.4    Plan for a conservation zone

Conservation of the historic areas has to be an integral part of the planning process. The qualities to be conserved include 'all the elements that express the character of the place'. These are identified as heritage components, which can be defined in terms of spatial extent.

(a) Qualities to be preserved
   - Urban patterns as defined by plots and streets
   - Relationship between buildings and green and open spaces
   - The formal appearance, interior and exterior of buildings as defined by scale, size, style, construction, materials, colour and decoration

- The relationship between the urban areas and its surrounding setting, both natural and material
- Various functions that the area has acquired over time

(b) Delineation of zones

It is clear from the statistics that two most critical things are the identification of ownerships and secondly the demarcation of exact boundaries on the map. The boundary delineation is a critical process and includes the following tasks:

- A detailed inventorying of the heritage components.
- Identifying the spatial extent of these components on plan
- Defining the extent of the zone based on the inventories and the historical studies
- Identifying a buffer around the zone for protect

The definition of the zones has to be based on understanding of the entity.

Understanding of Delhi as historic capitals and villages interlinked by numerous water bodies and streams gives us a better perspective for defining the 'zones'.

(i) Capitals

- Lal Kot, Quila Rai Pithora
- Siri
- Tughlaquabad, Nai Ka Kot, Adilabad
- Jahan Pahah: Chirag Delhi, Khirki, Begumpur, Hauz Rani
- Firoz Shah Kotla
- Purana Quila
- Sharhjahanabad: Chandni Chowk, Katra Neel, Bazar Lal Kuna, Dharampura, Jama Masjid, Red Fort, Lothian Road, Daryaganj
- Lutyens' Delhi: Connaught Place, Jantar Mantar, Central Vista, Bungalow Zone

(ii) Historic villages

- Nizamuiddin: Humayuns Tomb, Barapulla, Hazarat Nizamudding
- Mehrauli: Zafar Mahal, Mehrauli Bazaar, Qutb Complex.
- Hauz Khas

(iii) Clusters of monuments

- Lodhi Gardens
- Delhi Golf Club

This perspective also opens up the possibility of identifying more heritage zones based on the techniques of inventorying. Such as definition is a big exercise in itself and needs comprehensive understanding of the heritage resources of Delhi.

(iv) Urban villages

Many of the urban villages are historic, and remains of the past are worthy of conservation. However they have undergone various degrees of transformations. These have to be surveyed for their heritage resources.

## 3.4.1 Contents of the conservation plan

For any conservation plan participation of the occupants of the area is very crucial. Such plan may have following components:

(a) Heritage components and their ownership
(b) Traditional and historic housing stock
(c) Land use policy
(d) Physical infrastructure
(e) Traffic and transportation
(f) Information management
(g) Education and awareness
(h) Tourism
(i) Capacity building

'Capacity building' is the process and means through which individuals and organizations develop the necessary skills and expertise to manage their environmental and natural resources in a sustainable manner within their daily activities.

## 3.5 Master Plan 2021 proposals

For the first time Master Plan for Delhi 2021 included a separate and dedicated chapter on "conservation of built heritage" in the text of Master Plan, this chapter includes.

• *Conservation strategy:* A common conservation strategy for all the agencies concerned with protection of Delhi's built heritage is necessary. All the agencies should prepare appropriate action plans with the aim of framing policies and strategies for conservation. The strategy should include promotion of conservation of the civic and urban heritage, architecturally significant historical landmarks, living monuments, memorials and historical gardens, riverfront, city wall, gates, etc. Interaction and coordination between all these agencies must be part of overall strategy. All the agencies should follow common database, definitions and guidelines for development, redevelopment, additions alterations, repairs, renovations and reuse of the heritage buildings.

- *Heritage zones*: Heritage zone is an area, which has significant concentration, linkage or continuity of buildings, structures, groups or complexes united historically or aesthetically by plan or physical development. The following areas have been identified as heritage zones as indicated in the zonal plan.
    i. Specific heritage complex within Walled City of Delhi, Shahjahanabad.
    ii. Specific heritage complex within Lutyens' Bungalow Zone.
    iii. Specific heritage complex within Nizamuddin and Humayun's Tomb Complex.
    iv. Specific heritage complex within Mehrauli area.
    v. Specific heritage complex within Vijay-Mandal–Begumpur-Sarai Shahji–Lal Gumbad.
    vi. Specific heritage complex within Chirag Delhi.
- *Archaeological park*: Archaeological park in an area distinguishable by heritage resource and land related to such resources, which has potential to become an interpretive and educational resources for the public in addition to the value as a tourist attraction.

Though the priority is the historical structures and the built heritage, ecological and landscape aspects are not excluded.

All decisions regarding built heritage in general and archeological parks in particular should be based on evaluation of the pertinent aspects like form and design, materials and substance, use and function, traditions and techniques, location and setting, spirit and feeling and other internal and external factors.

The following areas have been designated as archaeological parks:
- i. Mehrauli Archaeological Park
- ii. Tughlazuabad Archaeological Park
- iii. Sultant Garhi Archaeological Park

Other areas can be added to the list on the basis of studies.

- Special conservation plans: Each local body/land owning agency should formulate "special development plans" for the conservation and improvement of listed heritage complexes and their appurtenant areas. Alteration or demolition of any listed heritage building is prohibited without the prior approval of the competent authority.

The development plans/schemes for such areas shall conform to the provisions, in respect of conservation of heritage sites including heritage buildings, heritage precincts and features areas.

## 3.6    Conclusion

The Master Plan 2021 has brought focus and vision with respect to conservation of built heritage. For the first time the idea and concept of heritage zone, archaeological park has been introduced in the Master Plan document. The scope of heritage encompasses monument along with linkages or continuity of buildings, structures or complexes united historically or aesthetically. Similarly archaeological park is an area distinguishable by heritage resource and land related to such resources. Inclusion of these entities in Master Plan document makes it potential area for protection, conservation and an integral part of planning process.

### Conservation of Delhi's built heritage

# Conservation of built heritage

## HERITAGE ZONES

The following areas have been identified as Heritage Zones:

- Walled City of Delhi, Shahjahanabad
- Central Vista
- Nizamuddin and Humayun's Tomb Complex
- Mehrauli area
- Vijay Mandal – Begumpur – Sarai Shahji – Lal Gumbad
- Chirag Delhi

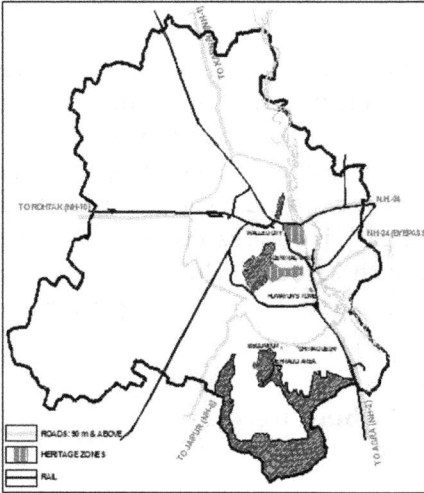

# An approach to conversation of built heritage
# Delhi master plan provisions

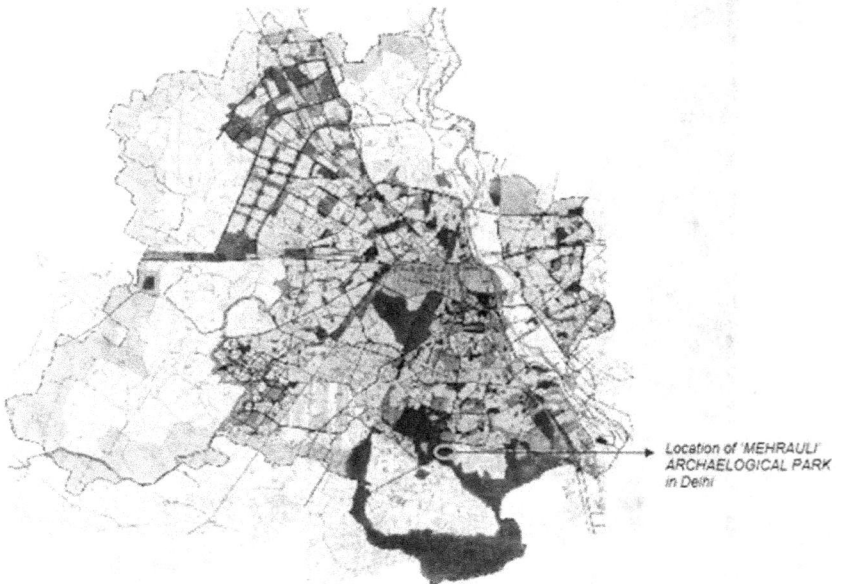

Location of 'MEHRAULI ARCHAELOGICAL PARK in Delhi

## Mehrauli... Historic background

Sketch of Environs of Delhi 1807

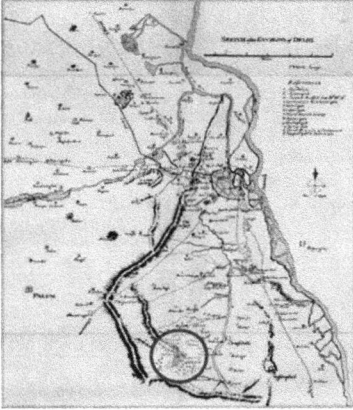

Source: ASI

Slave Dynasty

Mehrauli is a settlement that has evolved more than thousand years in succession.

Numerous major and minor historic monuments represent the architectural style of all major rulers of Delhi.

UNESCO World Heritage Site also forms the part of this area.

## Extents of Site...

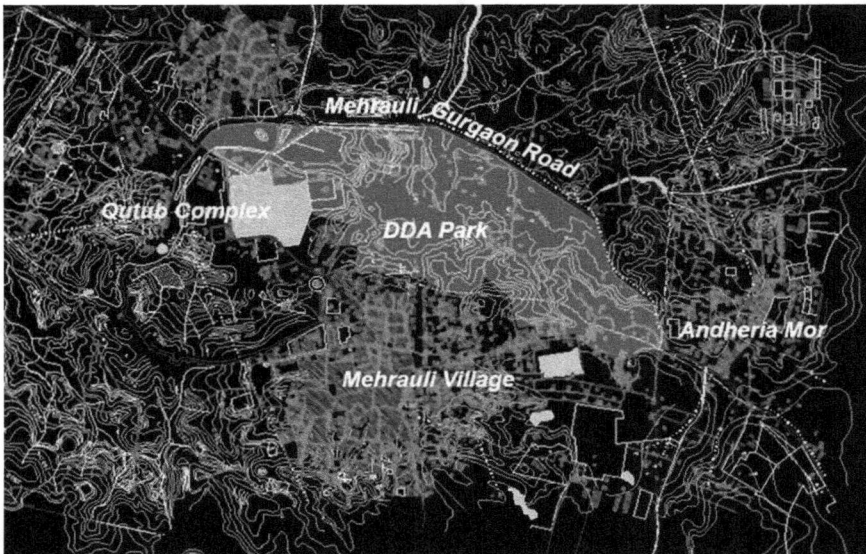

33

## Site potentials...   *Physiography and Hydrology*

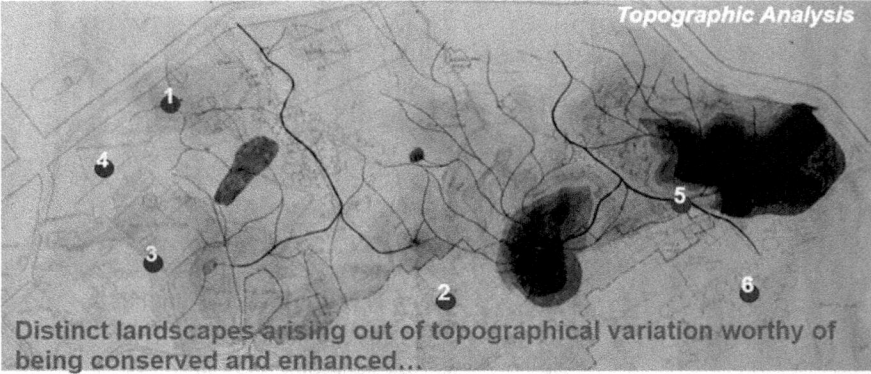

Topographic Analysis

Distinct landscapes arising out of topographical variation worthy of being conserved and enhanced...

1
Chhatri in front of Jamali Kamali...

2
Mehrauli village spread evenly over the ridge...

3
Quli Khan tomb & Qutub Complex sited over a plateau..

## Site potentials...   *Physiography and Hydrology*

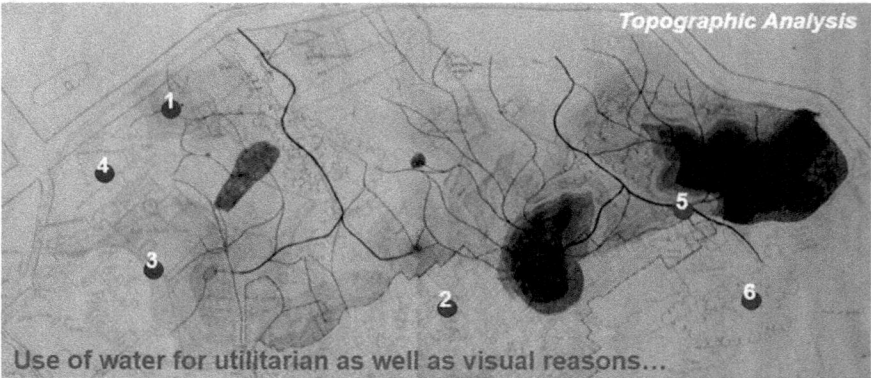

Topographic Analysis

Use of water for utilitarian as well as visual reasons...

4
Depressed land to the east of Dilkhusha, forming a bowl...

5
Jharna...
nestling between the valley

6
Hauz e Shamshi...
a man made reservoir

# Site potentials...

Landscape analysis

Chhattarpur Road

Qutb Complex

Mehrauli Village

Planted Vegetation

Historic orchards, formal gardens, fields and grazing lands, English landscape gardens, contemporary manicured gardens

...contemporary manicured gardens

# Site potentials...

*Historic structures*

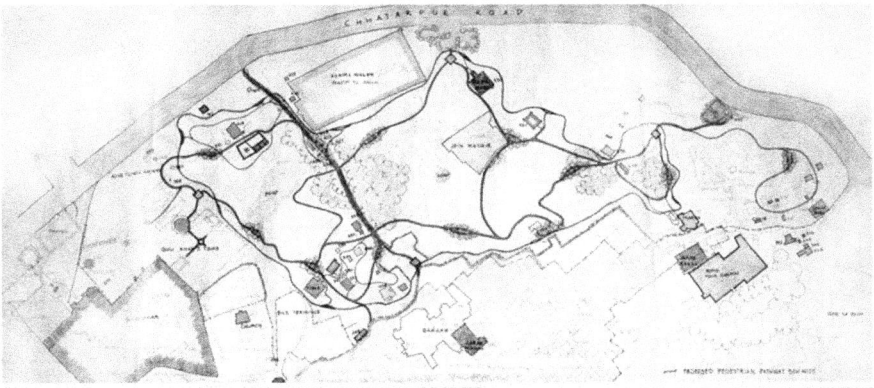

CHHATARPUR ROAD

Protected structures

...unprotected structures

An approach to conservation of built heritage: Delhi master plan provisions

**35**

## Depleted historic environment caused by

**Decay of historic buildings**

**Loss of fabric due to encroachment**

Within the forest area

Of/ around historic buildings

# Environmental degradation due to

● Loss of forest cover

● Lack of solid waste management

● Sewage in open natural drains

● Falling water table

● Defecation causing health hazards

# Cultural resource management plan...

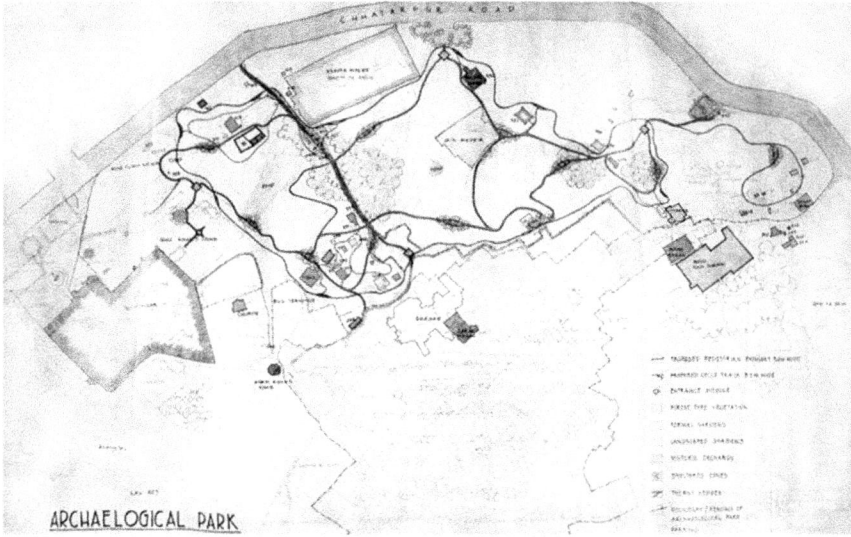

ARCHAELOGICAL PARK

Approved in the third meeting of Delhi Urban Heritage Foundation (DUHF)

## Heritage trail... *Intach in collaboration with DTTDC*

LEGEND

- Mehrauli settlement
- Bazaar street
- Forest land
- Manoured DDA parks
- Heritage planting / orchards
- Agricultural lands
- High points
- Water bodies
- Nala
- Historical monuments
- Monument clusters / complexes
- Proposed trail
- Starting points of trail

# Heritage trail...

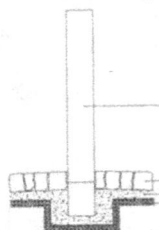

Existing

DQ Stone Rubble Paving of Av. Thickness 200 mm in Lime Mortar 1:4
100 mm Th Lean Lime Concrete 1:9:2:6
Levelled & Compacted Earth

- The path has been raised or lowered in the center as required to allow proper drainage of rain water

DQ Stone Rubble Paving of Av. Thickness 200 mm in Lime Mortar 1:4
100 mm Th Lean Lime Concrete 1:9:2:6
Levelled & Compacted Earth

**Detail 1: DQ stone paving**

50 mm Th Rough Chisel Dressed Red Sand Stone
100 mm Th Lean Lime Concrete 1:9:2:6
Levelled & Compacted Earth

**Detail 2: Red Sand Stone Paving**

Proposed

Levelled & Compacted Earth

**Detail 3: Leveled and Compacted Earth**

# Heritage trail...

Trail Markers

Monument Description Boards

The design approach designates three distinct zones:

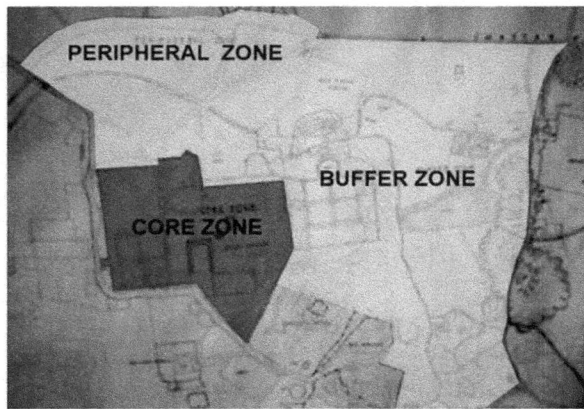

**Core Zone –**
Monument area, where interventions would be minimal

**Buffer Zone –**
comprising of open landscapes and greenery as an area of transition

**Peripheral Zone –**
where interventions will be allowed to facilitate visitors but controlled to ensure harmony with the overall environment

## Redefining missing links...

...existing openings closed

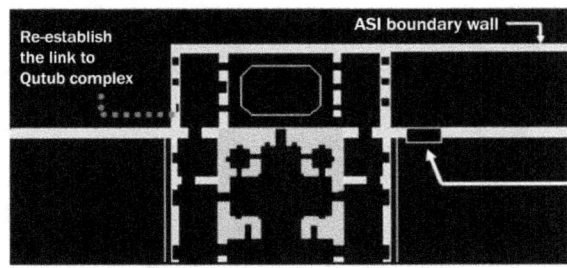

Metcalf's guest house infiltrating in the Qutub complex

## Redefining missing links...                                    *Concept*

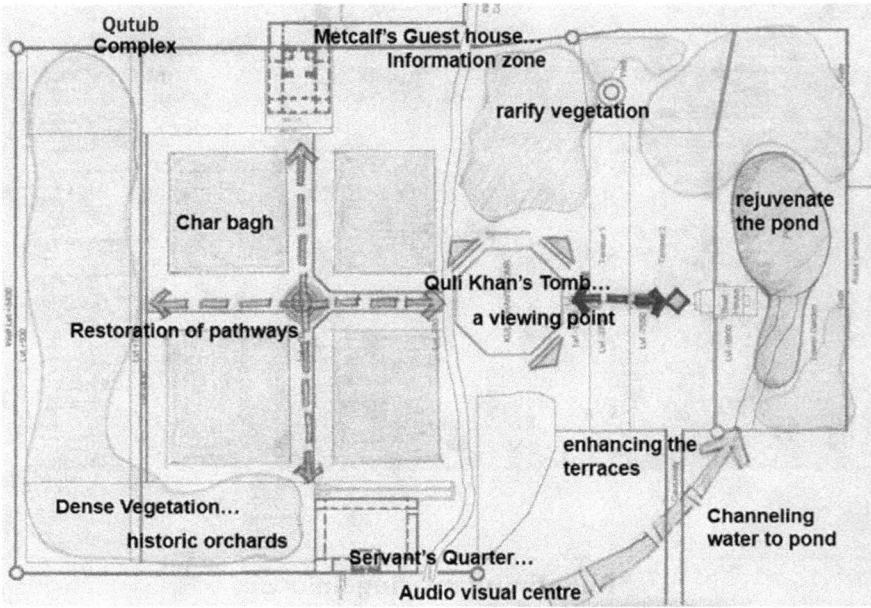

Qutub Complex

Metcalf's Guest house...
Information zone

rarify vegetation

Char bagh

rejuvenate the pond

Quli Khan's Tomb...
a viewing point

Restoration of pathways

enhancing the terraces

Dense Vegetation...
historic orchards

Channeling water to pond

Servant's Quarter...

Audio visual centre

## Redefining missing links...                                    *Concept*

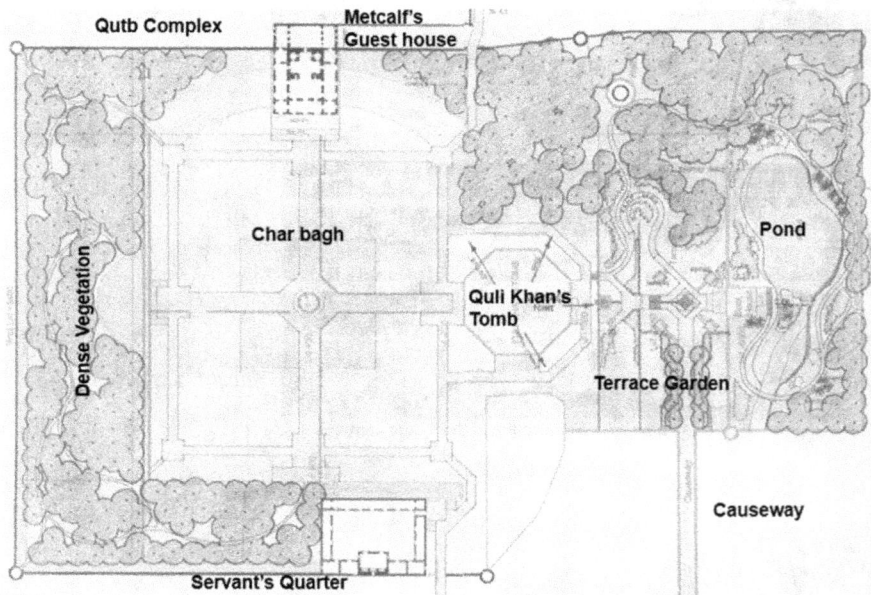

Qutb Complex

Metcalf's Guest house

Char bagh

Dense Vegetation

Quli Khan's Tomb

Pond

Terrace Garden

Causeway

Servant's Quarter

40

# References :

Master Plan For Delhi 1962

Master Plan For Delhi 2001

Master Plan For Delhi 2021

# 4

## Procedure-based planning: An approach for critical areas

### 4.1    Introduction

A new World Order is emerging because of the growth of India, China, Africa and South America. The traditional urban planning approach mostly borrowed from Western World has become less relevant in Indian context. Economic growth and technology are major factors behind the growth of cities due to substantial increase in income of people in countries like India. There is a desire and demand to lift the standard of all groups of the society.

Rising per capita income and resources for development of infrastructure, are the two factors driving policies and procedures of land use planning and master plan in India. For the first time planners are talking about economic growth, technology-driven mission and smart cities. So in the age of collaborations, Indian cities are under pressure to undertake drastic reforms in urban planning tools and techniques.

Indian cities and regions like National Capital Region have a role to play for unprecedented transformation of our cities, otherwise traditional urban planning may become less relevant if they do not adopt to changing situation.

Traditional planning promotes top–down approach of "controlled development of land" as per the land use plan, and space standards are giving way to "flexible procedures" which suit to requirement of the time.

There is paradigm shift which is compelling traditional planning methods to re-adjust its planning policies and procedures within the Master Plan and Zonal Plan framework to accommodate ground realities and local popular preferences. The concept of Master Plan and structure plan though being challenged, still remains the important planning tools to control future urban development which is crucial for the survival of Indian cities.

Roughly half of the world population will be living in the cities in the 21st century. The appropriate policies for the growth of world population and urbanization are crucial for sustainable development.

In order to avoid mismatch between physical development and economic development, critical analysis of planning policies and state of implementation through Master Plan document is required, taking into consideration the past experience and available technology.

## 4.2    Urban planning: Past experience

A broad review of various planning proposals and processes set during a period of 20 years of Master Plan for Delhi 2001 indicates that implementation of the proposals remains one of the most difficult tasks due to uncertainties of changing environment. It has been observed that the Master Plan proposals are successfully implemented where implementing agencies are clearly identified or implementing agencies are local bodies and MPD-2001 proposals have become part of annual action plan or budget of that agency. In most of the cases land was made available to these agencies by DDA. For example, land was allotted for hospitals, schools, fire station, police stations and sewage treatment plants and water treatment plants, etc.

Master Plan proposals remained unaddressed where jurisdiction of implementing agencies was not clear or there was no budget allocation for proposals.

## 4.3    New approach: Procedure-based planning

Master plan remains to be the only planning instrument which stood test of time despite criticism, severe limitations and slow pace of implementation. Master plan becomes a document which may bring reforms, flexibility and set implementable goals for urban planning process, with some innovative ideas and shift from 'standard based planning' to 'procedure based planning'. Current land use planning practice of prescribing uniform standards for all geographic areas irrespective of their socioeconomic status or local elements has resulted in incompatible land uses and unauthorized growth. Procedure-based planning integrates local issues like land ownership, socio-economic status and contribute to bottom–up approach to land use planning at zonal and master plan level, which is entirely top–down approach.

But it does not mean that current land use planning practice can be done away with. Judicious introduction of procedure-based planning for integration of local issues in the zonal and master plan framework is need of the hour.

Bottom–up procedures are successful for improving the quality of land use planning and resource management. Procedure-based planning aims at linking the micro level of management (i.e. farm, community land) and the level of policy making (zonal and master plan). In land use planning, the problem has more often been approached by studying the interactions between the biophysical and socio-economical elements of a land use system.

Procedure-based planning allows to:

- ascertain the representation of the important local planning issues at zonal development plan and master plan level;
- assure the feasibility of proposed local interventions by taking into account zonal development plan and master plan objectives and constraints (biophysical, socio-economical) as well as local knowledge, incentives and values; and
- provide local planners with decision-making tools for maximizing the potential of zonal development plan and master plan support (geo data, financial, organizational, etc.), checking the relevance of zonal and city level plans to local communities and reducing land use planning conflicts.

Procedure-based planning approach within overall framework of ZDP and MPD is most suitable for critical areas of urban policies and development where ZDP and MPD policies could not make impact at local level (land assembly, villages, unauthorized colonies, etc.).

## 4.4  Procedure-based planning for critical areas

These kind of new approaches are visible in master plan for Delhi 2021 document.

Following are few illustrations:

The Master Plan for Delhi with perspective up to year 2021 provides an opportunity to incorporate several innovations for the development of the National Capital. A critical reform has been envisaged in the prevailing land policy and facilitating public–private partnerships. MPD 2021 has included following as essential for land policy for future policy formulation:

- Review of the scheme of large-scale development and acquisition and its relevance in the present context;
- Alternative options for development of areas identified for urbanization in MPD 2021;
- Evolving a system under which planning for, and provision of basic infrastructure could take place simultaneously; and
- Involving the private sector in the assembly and development of land and provision of infrastructure services.

Procedure for land assembly is to be formulated and notified separately. It has not been made part of MPD document deliberately. Policies and procedures are liable to change from time to time to accommodate ground realities.

## 4.5     Procedure-based planning initiated in MPD 2021

*Local area plans*: Taking into consideration 73rd and 74th Constitution Amendment, the master plan for Delhi has introduced concept of local area plan. The master plan and zonal plan remain to be macro level plans which cannot respond to micro level ground realities. To absorb ground realities and formulate enforceable building bylaws, it will be necessary to focus on much smaller areas with more or less similar character and concerns. In other words areas with specific norms and standards need to be detailed out to prepare three-dimensional local area plans.

*Regularization of unauthorized colonies*: Master Plan for Delhi 2021 recognizes the problem of unauthorized colonies in Delhi. In the past policies, regularization was formulated as a corrective measure on and above prevailing master plan. For the first time MPD 2021 has clearly stated that all unauthorized colonies whether on private or public land regularization should be done as per government orders issued from time to time. For proper improvement of physical and social infrastructure, minimum necessary physical level of services and common facilities are to be provided. Master plan for Delhi provided reduced space standards for facilities taking into consideration difficulty in finding vacant plots for facilities in built-up areas. But actual procedure for regularization has been separated from MPD 2021 document. Thus, procedure-based planning as a part of MPD has been stated by the Master Plan for regularization of unauthorized colonies. As a follow-up action, the Ministry of Urban Development issued revised guidelines stating procedure for inviting applications from the associations of residents of unauthorized colonies for further processing of these applications by local bodies.

Further Ministry of Urban Development notified detailed procedure for regulation of unauthorized colonies on 24th March 2008 and 16th June 2008 for regularization of unauthorized colonies and issuing of 'provisional certificate for regularization' or in other words list of colonies which are eligible for regularization. Thus, MPD 2021 paved way for an era of procedure-based planning.

## 4.6     Procedure for regularization of unauthorized colonies

DDA notified Regulations of unauthorized colonies in Delhi under Section 57 of DD Act on 24 March 2008. This notification systematically prescribes procedure with step-by-step regulations for unauthorized colonies.

(i) Introduction clearly states the reasons for regularization of unauthorized colonies and the various definitions for terminology used in the Regulations;

(ii) Under criteria for regularization of unauthorized colonies and habitations, "cutoff date" for regularization is specified and criteria for regularization of unauthorized colonies as well as habitation that have come up as extensions of village abadies (population) and are outside the Lal Dora of village is also given. The Regulations also clearly state the colonies that are not to be considered for regularization, e.g. colonies falling in notified or reserved forests falling within the ROW or where 50 percent plots are un-built. Other criteria are violation of ancient monuments and archaeological projects and residential buildings used for non-residential purposes or unauthorized construction are not to be considered;

(iii) The following steps are to be followed for regularization after the notification:

- Registration of residents' society;
- Residents Society shall perform liaison work with concerned Agency in various matters pertaining to the regularization process, preparation of existing layout plan of the colony, it may voluntarily also submit proposal for improved layout plan, submission of list of members make available wherever possible, land to the concerned agencies for social infrastructure;
- List of documents to be submitted;
- Steps or procedure to be followed up by the Local body or government for regularization;
- A separate cell is to be created with the Local body or government to carry out the work. After the receipt of layout plan is submitted by the Residents' Society the local body will complete scrutiny in time bound manner.

Similarly, the boundaries are to be finalized in time bound manner by the government with the help of satellite imageries and aerial surveys;

After fixation of boundaries layout plan is to be forwarded to local body for approval;

- After the approval of LAP it will be forwarded to the Government for regularization; and
- Parameters and bases for regularization are:
  - title of land,
  - planning norms,

- mix use norms,
- recovery of land and development charges, and
- other miscellaneous things like grant of sanction or refusal, etc.

## 4.6.1    Special area and villages

MPD 2021 clearly states a procedure for dealing with special area and villages in addition to various planning provisions. Earlier master plans had given various provisions for these areas but the clear jurisdiction and responsibility of local bodies have been spelled out for the first time. The special area contains old city area, walled city and its extension, designated special area (Karol Bagh), which are mostly under the jurisdiction of Municipal Corporation of Delhi (MCD). To make special area plan practical and legitimate, this responsibility has been given to MCD.

## 4.6.2    Special area plans

MPD 2021 has defined special area and divided into three separate parts: namely (i) Walled City, (ii) Walled City and Extension, and (iii) Karol Bagh. On the basis of similarities in compact built form, narrow circulation space and low-rise high density developments, mainly accommodating residential, commercial both retail or wholesale and industrial uses.

The strategy is to provide suitable framework for allowing mix-use activities, household industries or outlets for specialized services, etc. Parking and open spaces have to be provided as per the norms, while reduced space norms for other facilities may be accepted. The redevelopment strategy should ensure modern services and amenities.

Regulations for special area shall be different from other areas. All these areas are to be brought with the planning purview. For this, the owners can jointly redevelop on the basis of the norms and regulations to be prescribed.

## 4.6.3    Villages

MPD 2021 has recognized that villages have undergone significant physical and functional transformations related with their specific location. Villages are characterized by a mix of different land uses and have similarities in compact built form, narrow circulation space and low-rise high-density developments. These mainly accommodate residential, commercial and industrial uses and function as a mix use.

Comprehensive schemes for the development of villages are to be prepared by the concerned local bodies with the aim of provision of optimal facilities and services within the abadis and integration with the surrounding areas. Development along the peripheries of the villages should be planned for the provision of services and green and open areas, circulation, etc., when preparing layout plans for urban extension areas. Reduced space standards are prescribed for provision of social and educational facilities. The facilities like community hall, dispensary, etc., may be grouped together depending on the availability land.

### 4.6.4    Mix use

• Mix use has emerged as a major provision of MPD 2021 due to emerging needs and requirement of people. Delhi, being the country's capital and an important centre of economic activity, has a large diversity in the typology of residential areas.Apart from the planned residential colonies built as part of Lutyens' Delhi as well as through the process of planned development undertaken by the Delhi Development Authority, there are authorized residential areas in the walled city, special areas and urban villages. Other planned areas include resettlement colonies and pre Delhi Development Colonies including post-partition rehabilitation colonies and pre-1962 residential colonies. There are also regularized unauthorized colonies as well as slums and jhuggi-jhompri clusters in various parts of Delhi; and

• MPD 2021 proposed to follow a differentiated approach in the application of the mixed-use policy in Delhi.The differentiated approach is based on categorization of colonies as adopted by MCD for unit area method of property tax assessment.

Subsequent to the notification of MPD 2021, Municipal Corporation of Delhi issued a public notice notifying 'Mixed Land Use as per MPD, 2021 and Payment of Mixed Land Use Charges'. Following are the excerpts:

As per Master Plan for Delhi 2021 under the Mixed Use Regulations, the following mixed use and commercial activities are permissible in residential premises (details as per clause 15 of MPD, 2021):

• *Mixed-use streets*: Details as per Clause 15.3, 15.4, 15.5, 15.6.1, 15.6.2 and 15.9 of MPD-2021;

• *Commercial streets*: Details as per Clause 15.12 of MPD-2021;

• *Small shops*: Details as per Clause 15.6.3 and 15.9 of MPD-2021;

• *Professional activities*: Details as per Clause 15.8 and 15.9 of MPD-2021;

• *Other activities*: Details as per Clause 15.7 and 15.9 of MPD-2021;

• *Group housing*: Details as per Clause 15.3.2 (4), 15.6.3 and 15.9 of MPD-2021;

- *Notified mixed-use streets* (including pedestrian streets) vide GNCTD notifications dated 15/09/2006 and 12/04/2007;
- *Notified commercial streets* (including pedestrian shopping streets) vide GNCTD notifications dated 15/09/2006 and 12/04/2007;
- *Small shops* of maximum 20 sq m area, trading in or dealing with the following items/activities, may be allowed on ground floor only, in residential premises, including in A and B category colonies;
- *Professional activity* subject to general terms and conditions specified in para 15.4 and 15.8 of Group Housing in all categories of colonies; and
- Other activities (As per MPD 2021, Clause 15.7).

## 4.6.5    Spot zoning

In April 2008, the Authority approved a policy for spot zoning of pre-existing cultural, religious (including spiritual) health care and educational institutions. The genesis of the concept of spot zoning comes from the recommendations of the Tejender Khanna Committee to protect genuine pre-existing institutions for this purpose. A committee was constituted under the Chairmanship of Commissioner (Planning), Chief Town Planner, TCPO, and Chief Town Planner of MCD to go into the concept of spot zoning. The Committee recommended that:

- The institutional activities which existed up to 1 February 2006 only are to be considered for regularization;
- The regularization shall be allowed on the lands which do not form part of the ridge, regional park, developed park, riverbed, gram sabha land or public land. Institutions on the lands affected by heritage zone, land required for master plan roads, service corridors, etc., shall not be regularized;
- The extent of buildable area shall be limited to the extent of MPD 2021 norms and the remaining surplus area shall be reserved for recreational green and open with a maximum 15 FAR subject to payment of levies, charges, other conditions as may be stipulated. Buildings so permitted will have to directly serve the principal objectives of the Institution;
- MPD 2021 under Clause 8 (2) permits certain public and semi-public facilities in residential and other use zones as a part of approval of lay out or as a case of special permission from the Authority;
- The regularization shall be subject to payment of all charges and

levies;

- The applicant will submit all the details of land ownership and area, built-up area, site plan indicating the location of building, building plans, etc., and
- The applications, thus, received will be examined by zone-wise committee for recommendations to the Authority.

The above steps suggest detailed procedure for integration at micro-level which is useful for the zonal plans. Contrary to the practice in our country, planning is not ruled by standards but by procedures in some of the developed countries. Planning practice in India inherited from colonial system of planning with rigid land use plan with well-defined functions, uniform standards and non-existence of flexibility.

Planning is considered an art, the planners has to have the freedom to propose an individual solution best adapted to the specific local conditions. Procedures do not prescribe uniform results; they ensure that for each individual situation the best possible results are identified.

## 4.7    Conclusions

Looking at the experience of other countries in procedure-based planning, one can say that innovative, people-oriented and procedure and trust-based planning system has resulted in saving of cost, regeneration of environment and improved living conditions for cities. Contrary to this, the Indian system of planning depends on standards rather than procedures which make it rigid, expensive and unimaginative.

Master plan stays despite of many odds. Urban planning needs to add wide range of planning tools like implementation mechanisms, short-term policies to meet with political exigencies and create interface between planning, implementing agencies and decision makers. Adding important planning tools like "procedure based planning" to the master plan document makes it implementable and result oriented.

Message is clear, flexible localized "procedure based planning" approach is necessary to integrate local issues like land assembly, mix use, regularization of unauthorized colonies and urban villages, etc., among themselves so that land use planning becomes practical and implementable.

# Spatial environmental planning: A German concept in urban and environmental planning

## 5.1 Introduction

The German Planning System has successfully integrated environmental objectives in physical planning, which is yielding high dividends on environment front. As a result of sustained campaign, at present drinking water needs of entire Germany is met through ground water and other local resources like river and lakes, thus, saving in massive cost of transportation of water and then in treating it. It has also enhanced the quality of air; water is flowing back in rivers and lakes. The author is of the view that the German experience has proved that it is much cost effective to protect our resources at the source than treating them at delivery point.

In 1970s, public awareness in Germany developed that "The environment is an asset worth protecting".

This awareness almost grew into a movement for improvement of spatial environment on the basis of sustainable development. Following factors also contributed for developing such public opinion.

- Irreversible damage caused to historic buildings, health and nature during development became a major concern among people.

- Policy makers at national level started thinking as to how can economic growth and prosperity be compatible with sustainable use of natural resources. High level of energy consumption raised doubts as to whether current production methods and lifestyle could be maintained. Doubts were raised about usefulness of nuclear power plants as disposal of waste is one of the major hazards. In fact many nuclear power plants are shut down in Europe.

- UN Conference on 'Environment and Development' in Rio de Janeiro in 1992 spelled out 'Agenda 21' for development, based on principles of environmental conservation, as growth and consumption is coming up against limits. What the richest 10% of the world population consumes in energy, land, water, air and other natural assets directly or indirectly, cannot be extended to the 90% without the Earth collapsing ecologically. Gradually and firmly a consciousness developed that "the days of the century of economic development are numbered, whether we like it or not, we are entering the "Century of the Environment".

## 5.2 Planning concepts based on environmental consideration

The German administration, with their elaborated planning system, availed a tool such as Environmental Impact Analysis (EIA) for projects as well as for spatial co-ordination and integration of environmental considerations. To use the spatial planning system for comprehensive environmental management was considered the most promising approach and consequently pursued by the German environmental administration. Therefore, from the beginning the German environmental administration was well aware of the structural unsuitability of EIA within the German system. The shortcomings of EIA, such as being a reactive instrument, coming only after the project idea are already very far advanced (and cannot be changed or sited elsewhere) or the lack of co-ordination in all existing EIA systems was only too obvious. Consequently, the German environmental administration opted for further developing and using the existing (spatial) planning system as an instrument to protect the environment in a comprehensive, holistic manner and integrate EIA procedures into the spatial planning systems. As a consequence of this, environmental objectives play a predominant role in spatial planning:

- Development of modern planning tools for spatial environmental planning for urban as well as rural planning, successfully incorporating environment into spatial planning, using spatial planning to protect environment as well as to use environment to strengthen spatial planning;
- Development of landscape planning as the ecological spatial planning system to restore and maintain the ecological balance of all rural lands which are predominantly under agricultural use (Figs. 5.1 to 5.5);
- Development of a comprehensive system of regionalised air quality management focusing on 'hot spots';
- Effective forest protection for a sustainable use for forest product, as a local climate buffer and against floods, avalanches, erosion and landslides introduced and effective since medieval times;
- Effective rehabilitation or restoration of water quality of large lakes (Bavarian lakes), streams (nallah) and rivers, and groundwater resources (the main drinking water source in Germany)

**Figure 5.1** The renaturation of a waterway in an urban setting

## 5.3 Effectiveness of German planning system

- *Spatial planning as major tool:* The German decision to develop spatial planning as a major tool for "preventive environmental protection" is clearly showing results and seems more effective than EIA. This was effectively supported by declaring environmental protection goals as guiding factor for spatial development.

**53**

- *Decentralised execution power:* In Germany, execution is normally delegated to the lowest possible level. Licensing of industries is granted at the taluka (county) level. This not only resulted in short lines of command and technical as well as local conversance of the executing authority but also freed the higher levels from technical tasks, leaving them to their main job, i.e. guiding development.

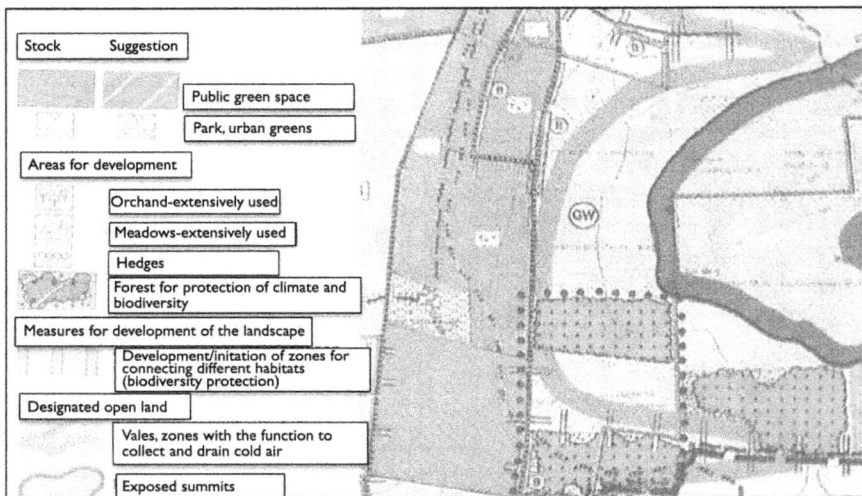

**Figure 5.2** 'Landscape management development' concept

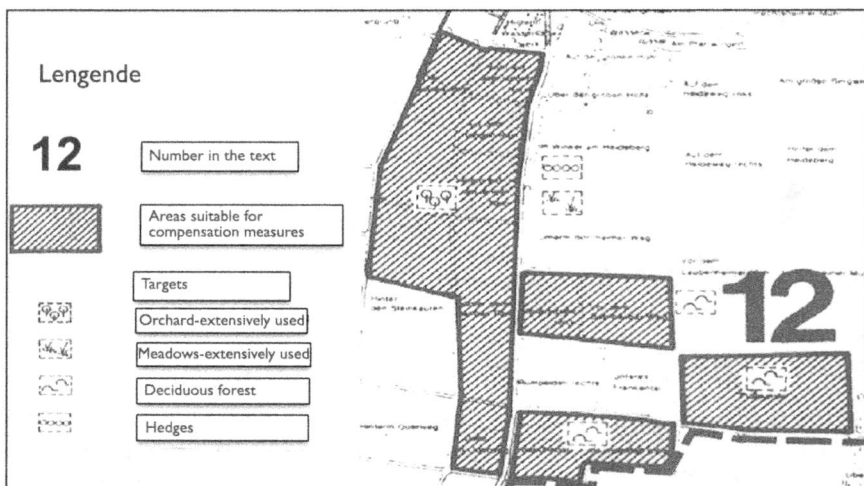

**Figure 5.3** Survey map of compensation areas based on the development concept

Legende

| | |
|---|---|
| | Areas for forest/planned deciduous forest |
| | Limits of areas for measures to protect, manage and develop nature and landscape (§5 para 2 No 10 building law) |

Purpose
existing planned

| existing | planned | |
|---|---|---|
| | | Orchard-extensively used |
| | | Meadown-extensively used |
| | | Hedges |
| LEF | | Areas for compensation and contingency measures |
| ооо | | Zones for "Green Networks" |

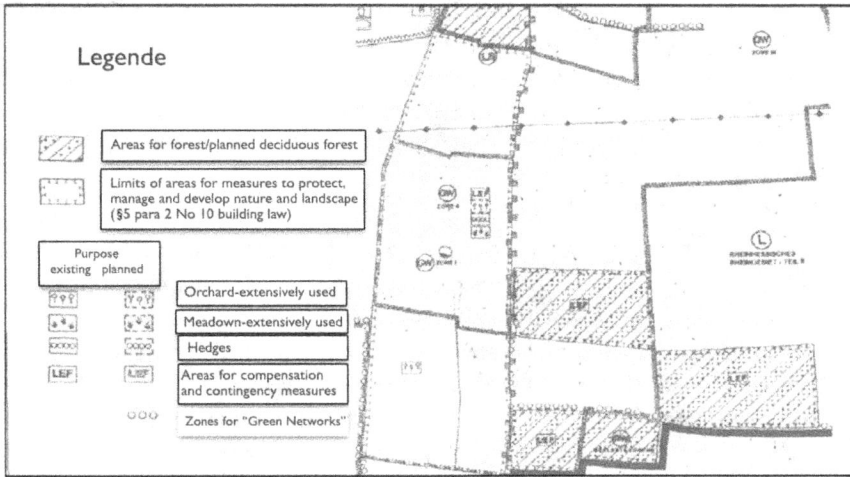

**Figure 5.4** Integration of recommendations into the 'draft land use plan'

## 5.4 Planning as a "Conflict coordination theatre"

The main feature of spatial planning in Germany consists of its perception primarily as 'Conflict Coordination Theatre.' Consequently, spatial planning is also called co-coordinative planning (in contrast to sector planning). The role of planning is not to ensure coordinated implementation of plans but implementation – as far as spatial plans are concerned – is neither the purpose nor the end of a plan. The plan itself is a platform wherein the demands for land from different social groups has been coordinated, balanced and finally agreed in a form of a sound integrated concept which is accepted within the society. In other words, the spatial plan represents the social consensus how the land should be used.

## 5.5 Planning in Germany: Standards versus procedures

*Planning as an art.* Planning in Germany is not ruled by standards but by procedures. Standards have their place in execution of measures; in planning they are considered as too static. Planning is considered an art; the planner has to have the freedom to propose an individual solution best adapted to the specific local conditions. Procedures do not prescribe uniform results; they ensure that for each individual situation the best possible result is identified. This 'softness' of planning is in fact its strong point.

*Planning by associations.* In many fields planning is not executed by governmental authorities but by associations or co-operatives. Leaving planning to the primarily concerned but under governmentally controlled procedures results in sound and, in particular, accepted plans.

*The effectiveness of vertical and horizontal coordination.* Most important are procedures in guiding the plan co-ordination. Even if these procedures are cumbersome and lengthy, they ensure optimal consideration of all sectors and results in sound integrated concepts.

*Employment of "soft" planning tools.* Germany has developed a toolbox of "soft" planning tools, mostly resource evaluation inventories to be used for planning purposes. Their use is not compulsory but each planning authority is aware of them and uses them during plan preparation. Example is the so-called Biotop Mapping, an inventory of all ecologically significant habitats available in a scale of 1: 5.000 for the whole country.

*The pragmatism of approaches and tools.* Most planning approaches and solutions are pragmatic and directed towards solving problems. Behind all spatial plans stand the simple policy: Provide more development potential (sites) than possibly demanded. This will ensure that the plan controls development in the desired way provided that the selection of offered development sites is based on environmental considerations.

## 5.6    Planning as a "bottom–up process"

* Evolving of (spatial) planning at higher planning levels start from the municipal level in a bottom–up process. Industrialisation with its mushrooming urbanisation clearly showed the need for coordinated and integrated spatial planning beyond and above the local level. Consequently, in 1919 the first Regional Planning Association (SVR) was established in the Ruhr district, then the largest industrial region in Europe. Important to note that the organisational form chosen was that of an association – members are mainly from the municipalities and *talukas* – and not a centralised governmental authority. This Regional Planning Association has been very successful in guiding settlements development in Germany's largest industrial area since its inception.

* This organisational form of planning associations – basically a bottom–up approach – has been repeated throughout the country. Regional planning at district level was introduced some 30 years back. Regional plans are prepared for several themes and are guiding the further detailing of plans at the municipal level.

## 5.7    Environmental objectives

Environmental objectives play a dominant role even in the federal spatial planning framework law. Often half of all spatial development objectives are explicit environmental objectives or related to them. The general objectives of incorporating environmental considerations into spatial plans include:

- Use of the land according to its natural (environmental) suitability in a way that the use is not adversely affecting its natural conditions and/or its natural functions on a sustainable basis;
- Restoration, rehabilitation or sanitation of lands and land-based natural resources already degraded by human activities;
- Preservation of ecologically sensitive and important lands respectively eco-systems with the effect that their functions for nature as well as society are sustainable and preserved;
- Preservation and/or management of land-based natural resources such as water (e.g. ground water).

This is carried out within the German spatial planning system which consists of mainly three levels:

- State level planning (in state-level plans or programmes)
- Regional (district) planning (in regional plans)
- Municipal planning (in master plans and layout plans)

All plans at all levels have in common the following:

- They provide development potential and direct its development in an environmentally compatible manner.
- Implementation is not a direct part of the plans; its main function is development guidance.
- All plans are thoroughly coordinated vertically (within the spatial planning hierarchy) as well as horizontally (with all concerned sector plans and programmes) following the counter-current principle (simultaneous co-ordination bottom–up and top–down).
- The upper planning level guides development at lower planning level, while the lower planning levels provide input into the plans development at higher planning levels.
- All plans summarise the socially accepted future demand for land and resources identified in a democratically organised process involving all social groups and the general public.

## 5.8   Water protection zone

German administration believes in protecting potable water at source rather than treating water after it gets polluted. Such protection measures are cost effective and environment friendly. Out of this philosophy, a concept of "Water protection zone" is developed and used as planning tool. This planning tool regulates the use of land with important functions mainly for water supply. Protected are ground water resources near wells serving potable water supply systems but also surface waters. Within a water protection zone, all activities that eventually may lead to contamination of water are regulated and eventually prohibited. The zones are classified according to the protection need expressed in percolation distance from the source to be protected. In the strictest protection zone, even access is prohibited and only allowed to the workers of the waterworks (Fig. 5.5).

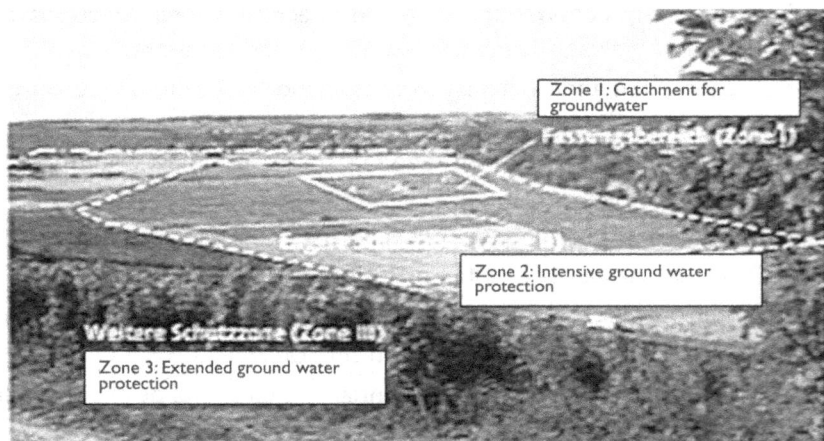

**Figure 5.5** Water protection zone

In principle, the technical plan preparation usually involves the following principal steps:

- Description of the existing situation (existing land use, planning restrictions, etc.),
- Identification of demand and its translation into required sites for residential, industrial development need,
- Assessment of site development potential and constraints for different uses based on site potential assessment (this is the main step where environmental considerations are incorporated),
- Preparation of a first plan concept for first discussions.

## 5.9 Management of river's wholesomeness by co-operative

A bold, innovative approach to manage water resources introduced 100 years ago is still working effectively today. At the first instance, task was of defining and detailing of water quality management objectives. Following objectives were outlined:

- Managing river flow in such a manner that all uses remain possible throughout the year, even in dry spells.
- Managing river quality so that hygienic safety and drinking water production could be maintained in a sustainable manner.
- Direct siting of water polluting activities (industries etc.).
- Identifying fees to be paid by the members of the co-operative for all necessary operational expenses to do the job. Manage its own affairs without interference from the bureaucracy to achieve the objectives promulgated by the law.

Whether to have one central treatment facility or many decentralised ones, whether to rule and control by standards or procedures or only by mutual consent among the members was left to the cooperative to decide without external (governmental) interference. This concept turned to be a path breaking towards success.

## 5.10    Planning and implementation of industrial estates

For planning and implementation of industrial estates, total evaluation criteria are adopted on the following basis:

(1)  Sensitivity to environment planning

(2)  Sensitivity to resources

All the environmental criteria are included in EIA. Existing eco-systems like marshy land, the system of rivulets and floodplains, forest with special importance are studied. In German context, the river network is the backbone of the development of the new industrial estates, in addition to connectivity by road, rail and air. Special features, on the basis of environmental factors, are:

- rain-water harvesting,
- area for compensatory measures,
- creation of phases of construction.
- For planning purposes, terrain, contours and open spaces with special functions are studied and superimposed on each other. Then constructible area is defined. State-level industrial planning is further followed and adopted at district and local levels. In addition to usual procedure and policy consent, procedure is innovative

where consent of public and stake-holders is taken before plan is finalised. Due to this involvement of all concerned, plan is respected and followed by all.

- One of the important aspects of industrial planning estates is regional context and ecological factors. Due to this reason not only industrial plots are generated but community is also benefited in terms of water bodies, forests and nature.

- Appreciable feature is: 'conflicts between various sectors' are mentioned with instrument to solve conflicts through discussion with stakeholders. Recycling of abandoned industrial sites for ecological enhancement and urban development has helped to create needed infrastructure and employment opportunities for communities. Creation of buffer zones helps to delineate and maintain environment zones.

- In case of Munich-burg Industrial Estate in Germany, two neighbouring municipalities have formed co-operative to invest money and share revenues. This concept can be considered in Indian context as towns are merging and administrative boundaries are vanishing.

- Concept of 'Mitigation Planning' and 'valuation of the state before impact' is a good idea for adoption in Indian context to avoid litigation in future. In this method, not only quantification of flora and fauna is done but protected species are also considered. In return, communities get parks, water bodies and improved environment.

- Integration of all traffic modes and creation of parking facilities at airport or any activity node is an example of planning with focus on people. Rainwater harvesting has helped nearby farmers to irrigate their land. Due to such benefits, resistance from neighbours is minimal to such projects.

- Creation of buffer zones, conflict management and instruments for solving conflicts through public participation are ideas for Indian planning as it will help to avoid litigations and delays. Moreover, it will create a sense of belongingness to a plan.

- Regional plan defines connectivity of highways, railways, air link and regional ecosystem including river system, etc. Thus, areas for local planning are left to local bodies. For locating industries and environmental protection in India, following measures are suggested:

  - Mechanism of regional planning needs to be strengthened.

- Approach of 'bottom–up' planning instead of top–down planning at local level may be appropriate, as it will lessen conflict between regional plan and local plan.
- Environmental information database and identification of zones suitable for industrial siting with spatial consideration of development of an area shall prove useful in enhancing success ratio of developmental plans of various sectors.

# 5.11 Urban renewal programs

Urban renewal programmes are sine qua non with any urban development, in order to stop decay of the core city or old areas. Core city or old areas have following problems:

- Old buildings in dilapidated conditions
- Narrow roads
- Lack of parking spaces
- Lack of open spaces, parks and children play areas
- Community places
- Physical and social infrastructure
- Traffic problems
- Social and cultural spaces

Any urban renewal programme has to address above concerns. In addition to above, these areas have historical buildings, buildings of cultural heritage which need to be conserved. In general, total environment needs improvement. In German context, urban renewal is at three levels:

- City development and rehabilitation programme
- Village level renewal plans for generation of economic activity for dying villages
- Integration of natural features like rivers, flood plains and water bodies

Special features of urban renewal are:

- Increase in land consumption (space occupation, increase in standards of living)
- Increase in resource consumption

In urban renewal, most important aspect is 'public participation'. Plans based on public participation are welcome by residents and public. Municipality as well as the state play important role not only in formulation of plans, but also play an active role in financing the development. Most unique feature is financial incentives and investment to create open spaces and infrastructure by buying old houses and removing them to create parks, parking areas and roads, etc. Urban renewal also offers an opportunity for up-gradation of old infrastructure like water supply lines, sewer lines, fire-fighting measures, etc.

- The partnership approach to urban renewal between local body and public is a very good concept. Governments at three levels are contributing catalyst investments, acting as a facilitator for urban renewal which is to be taken up by the owners\ tenants jointly. Instead of going by the procedures, the approach is found flexible enough to suit the individual situations, thus focusing on the end result.

- Urban renewal programmes are not only restricted to cities but also prepared for villages to rejuvenate them by creating economic development in recreational sectors, e.g. Franconia Lake District, an artificial lake or bird sanctuary created as recreation resource. Thus, it has created economy for villages, balance in regional development and sustainable ecological system.

- Public participation and bottom–up approach at local level have created high degree of awareness among the people and the residents (Fig. 5.6).

**Figure 5.6** Urban renewal: Creation of open spaces

## 5.12    Conclusion

The German experience of connecting environmental management with spatial planning is an interesting approach towards a preventive environmental policy. It is worthwhile to study this approach and find inspiration for planning environment related policies for developing countries. Neither can it be said nor can it be recommended that German planning policies and practices can be adopted similarly in Indian conditions, but environmental ideas and innovative policies/procedures are worth trying within the existing planning framework.

# 6

# Monitoring and implementation of the master plan policies in Delhi

## 6.1　Introduction

Town planning is the British legacy to India. After independence we continued to pursue planning, notably through master plans. Indeed, master plans have played an important role in guiding and shaping urban development of cities in India. More than one thousand master plans have been prepared in the last five decades, but record of implementation is less than encouraging. Consequently, momentum in favor of limited utility of master plans seems to be gathering in many influential policy circles.

This chapter examines how far Delhi Development Authority in Delhi has been able to implement the Master Plan for Delhi 2001.

## 6.2　Master Plan for Delhi, 1981–2001

Master plan for Delhi has remained a pioneering document in the field of urban planning in India. With vast experience of plan preparation and implementation, Delhi Development Authority published the second master plan for Delhi in 1991 with the perspective up to year 2001. Implementation remains one of the most difficult tasks of all due to uncertainties of changing environment. Even the Master Plan 2001 has acknowledged this fact in its preamble.

"...there are a number of stages from enunciation of planning principle to its accomplishment. All the above postulates during the process needed adequate acceptance, detail planning and execution; in fact during implementation, they sometimes tend to suffer some loss at every stage. The end result in some spheres has, therefore, been insubstantial. There are other issues of central importance like rapid urban population and employment growth, land use permissibility, land use intensity, informal sector and incompatible uses which overwhelmed the Master Plan in the process of its implementation".

## 6.3      Monitoring and implementation

Due to various factors related to non-implementation of the master plan, the concept of structure plan came into existence. Structure plan is flexible and largely a policy document. But preparation of a structure plan and process of approval is also time consuming. There is a criticism against structure plan also that is structure plans are too much flexible and therefore does not guide physical development. The concept of structure plan is being questioned in the country of its origin itself.

At the turn of the century, it is an opportunity to look back at the concept of master plan as well as structure plan and our experiences of plan implementation in the last four to five decades. Demand in contemporary planning is dynamism, quick adjustment with market forces, and approaches that transform policies into land use modules. Rigidity of planning processes must go and be replaced with accountability and transparency. A discussion of this topic can be open ended. Let us confine our discussion around the proposals of Master Plan for Delhi 2001 (MPD-2001) and level of implementation achieved. Perspective period of 20 years is over and it is right time to prepare a balance sheet for MPD-2001. MPD-2001 has the following components.

- Existing scenario, policies and projections related to population in regional context and projection of demand, requirement for space, land, physical/social infrastructure and land use plan.
- Population norms and space standards.
- Development code, permissibility and monitoring framework.

There is no standard method for evaluation of MPD proposals. The author has tried to put all proposals for urban extension in a tabular format for each aspect of MPD-2001 along with agency responsible for implementation. Status of implementation has been indicated in remarks columns. The picture emerged is given in Table 6.1 below.

**Table 6.1** Proposals of Master Plan for Delhi-2001 and its implementation in the urban extension

| S. no. | Proposal of MPD-2001 | Urban aextension / project of DDA | Government agency responsible for implementation | Status |
|---|---|---|---|---|
| 1. | 2. | 3. | 4. | 5. |
| **I. Industry** | | | | |
| | (i) Samaipur Badli Area | Rohini | Delhi Govt. | Land not available |
| | (ii) Extensive Industrial Area G.T. Road Group I | | Delhi Government / DDA | Non-confirming industries being shifted on the basis of Supreme Court of India orders |
| | (iii) Cotton, wool, silk, synthetic fiber, textile product | | | Service centers in Rohini, Dwarka and Narela |
| | (iv) Furniture, fixture, other wood + paper product | | | |

Contd...

| S. no. | Proposal of MPD-2001 | Urban aextension / project of DDA | Government agency responsible for implementation | Status |
|---|---|---|---|---|
| 1. | 2. | 3. | 4. | 5. |
| **II. Trade and commerce** | | | | |
| | (i) One sub-central business district (sub-CBD) proposed in urban extension | No such proposal | DDA | |
| | (ii) Eight district centers to be developed in urban extension | • Rohini-3 (Ph. I and II) | DDA | Planning / Execution stage |
| | | I (Ph. III) | | Planning stage |
| | | 4 Total | DDA | |
| | | • Dwarka – Linear I Distt. Centre | | |
| | | • Narela –2 + I non- hierarchy commercial center | | |
| | | • Vasant Kunj – Phase II – I | | |
| | (iii) 40 community centers to be developed in urban extension | • Narela – 10 | DDA | • Not yet planned |
| | | • Dwarka – 6 | | • Three are at design stage |
| | (iv) Organized informal sector, eating places in urban extension such places could be part of planned development on the norm of one sub cluster for one lakh population at community level | • Near TV Tower Pitampura | DDA | Not yet planned, however 3 acres have been reserved for cultural complex |
| | | • Behind Andrews Ganj (South) | HUDCO | Being developed |
| | | • CC near Mandi House | L & DO | Being developed |
| | | • Near Sub CBD Trans Yamuna Area | DDA | Being developed |
| | (v) Regional distribution Markets | | | |
| | East – Near Patpar Ganj and on Loni Road | Gazipur | DDA | Loni Road land not available |
| | South – Near Madan Pur Khadar | South | DDA | Most of the land with UP Govt. Dwarka-Land acquired. |
| | South West in Urban | Dwarka | DDA | Narela being planned however out of 350 hectares only 57 hac. Has been planned. |
| | Extension North In Urban Extension | Narela | DDA | |
| | (vi) Regional cum local distribution market | | | |
| | • Sub CBD (Shahdara) South | | DDA | Wholesale market planned for electronics etc. developed |
| | • Okhla | | DDA | Developed |
| | • Rohtak Road District Centre (North) | | DDA | Not developed |
| | • Shivaji Place District Centre (North) | | Slum & JJ | Being developed |
| | • Wazirpur District Centre | | DDA | Developed |
| | • Rohini District Centre | | DDA | Developed |
| | • Markets of 8–10 hectares in urban extension | | DDA | |
| | • Fodder market in rural areas | | DDA / Delhi Govt. | Whole grain market developed in Narela. To be planned by Delhi Govt. as part of growth centres |
| **III. Government Offices** | | | | |
| | (i) Delhi Admin. District Courts | Rohini | Delhi Govt. | Under construction |
| | (ii) Near Saket District Centre – 7 hac. | Saket | Delhi Govt. | Land allotted adjoining to Distt. Centre |
| | (iii) Near Sub CBD Shahdara – 3.0 hac. | | Delhi Govt. | Being developed |

| S. no. | Proposal of MPD-2001 | | Urban aextension / project of DDA | Government agency responsible for implementation | Status |
|---|---|---|---|---|---|
| 1. | 2. | | 3. | 4. | 5. |
| | (iv) Outer Ring Road and Western Yamuna Canal junction – 3.0 hac. | | Rohini | Delhi Govt. | Land allotted for jail & constructed |
| | (v) Near District Centre in South West (Urban Extn.) – 3 hac. | | Dwarka | Delhi Govt. | Land allotted in Dwarka |
| **IV. Transportation Network** | | | | | |
| | A. Rail | | | | |
| | (i) Ring Railway Stations to be shifted | | | | |
| | From | To | | | |
| | Chanakyapuri | Near Moti Bagh | | Railways | Yet to be executed |
| | Pragati Maidan | Bhairon Road | | Railways | Yet to be executed |
| | Tilak Bridge | Hans Bhawan | | Railways | Yet to be executed |
| | (ii) Broad Gauge link between Gurgoan and Kirti Nagar | | Railways | | Accomplished |
| | (iii) New Railway Stations are required at Inderpuri, Rampura, Gandhi Nagar, Shyam Lal College, Shakarpur | | Railways | | Yet to be done |
| | (iv) Metre Gauge terminal would be shifted from Delhi Main Railway station to the proposed integrated transport terminal at Bharthal, Dwarka | | Dwarka | Railways | Land available |
| | B. Rail Passenger Terminals | | | | |
| | (a) Four Metropolitan Passenger terminals proposed | | | | |
| | • Trans Yamuna | | Anand Vihar | Railways | Land handed over to Railways |
| | • Okhla / Tughlakabad | | | Railways | Being developed at Nizamuddin by Railways |
| | • Barthal to cater West Delhi and part of Urban Extension | | Dwarka | Railways | The land is acquired by DDA |
| | (b) Second entry to Delhi Main Railway Station | | | Railways | Functioning |
| | (c) M.R.T.S (Ph- I) (Metro Rail) | | | DMRC | Under implementation |
| **V. Infrastructure** | | | | | |
| | A. Infrastructure (Physical) Water Trearment Plants | | | | |
| | - Chandrawal I and II | | | MCD | Completed |
| | - Wazirabad | | | MCD | Completed |
| | - Hyderpur I and II | | | MCD | Constructed |
| | - Shahdara | | Rohini | MCD | Land allotted |
| | - New plants in N.W. Delhi | | | MCD | 9th Five Year Plan |
| | - Okhla | | | MCD | Completed |
| | -Rainy wells | | | MCD | Five rainy wells in Alipur block |
| | Min. domestic water supply required 135 litres (30 gallons) | | | | (Add. WTP came up in NANGLOI) |
| | Seweage Treatment Plants | | | | |
| | -Okhla | | | MCD | |
| | -Keshopur | | | MCD | |
| | -Coronation | | | MCD | |
| | -Rithala | | | MCD | Functioning |
| | -Shahdara (Kondli) | | Rohini | MCD | |
| | -New Plant in West Delhi | | Rohini Ph. IV | MCD | |
| | -New Plant in North Delhi | | | MCD | |
| | | | Narela and Alipur | MCD | |
| | | | Rohini | MCD | Not commissioned |
| | | | Najafgarh | MCD | |

*Contd...*

| S. no. | Proposal of MPD-2001 | Urban aextension / project of DDA | Government agency responsible for implementation | Status |
|---|---|---|---|---|
| 1. | 2. | 3. | 4. | 5. |
| | Solid Waste | | | |
| | The sites proposed for sanitary landfill area | | | |
| | -Site near Hasthal village in West Delhi | | MCD | Completed |
| | -Site on Ring Road near village Sarai Kalekhan | | MCD | Being used for land filling |
| | -Site in the North West Delhi | Near Sanjay Gandhi Tpt. Terminal | MCD | Being used for land filling |
| | -Site near Gazipur Dairy Farm | MCD | | Completed |
| | -Trans Yamuna Area | | Nil | Nil |
| | -Site near Timarpur existing landfill | | MCD | Completed |
| | -Site near Gopalpur village in North Delhi | | MCD | Completed |
| | -Site near Jahangirpur | | MCD | Completed |
| | B. Infrastructure (Social) | | | |
| | -19 fire stations in the urban extension would be required | | Delhi Govt. | 4 allotted in Dwarka & four provided in Narela |
| | Education | Urban Extension | | |
| | -Primary School | 762 | | |
| | -Sr. Sec. School | 508 | | About 250 sites provided in Dwarka, Rohini & Narela |
| | -Integrated School | | | 15 provided in Dwarka, 20 provided in Narela |
| | -Technical education center | 9 | Delhi Govt. | 2 provided in Dwarka, 2 in Narela |
| | -University Campus | 1 Dwarka | Delhi Govt. | Land allotted in Dwarka to Indraprastha University |
| | Health | | | |
| | -General Hospitals | 12 | GNCTD | Gen. Hospitals provided in Dwarka, Rohini & Narela |
| | -Intermediate Hospital A | 39 | | 4 Gen. Hospitals provided in Narela 8 provided in Dwarka 10 provided in Narela |
| | -Intermediate Hospital B | 39 | | 8 provided in Dwarka 10 provided in Narela |
| | -Nursing Homes (Private) | 75 | | 108 functioning: 6 Polyclinic provided in Dwarka 20 provided in Narela (Nursing Homes) |
| VI. Others | | | | |
| | - Police Station | 44 | | 7 handed over in Dwarka 20 provided in Narela |
| | - Fire Station | 19 | | 4 handed over in Dwarka 4 provided in Narela |
| | - District Jail | 5 | | Rohini, near Dwarka & TYA land allotted |
| | - Head Post Office | 6 | | Part of Community Centers 4 |
| | - Telephone Exchange | 9 | | Provided in Narela, Rohini & Dwarka |
| | -Department of Telegraph | 5 | | Provided in Dwarka and Narela |
| | -L.P. G. Godown | 25 | | Provided in Narela, Dwarka & Rohini |

It is observed that although MPD 2001 provided for a monitoring framework, it lacked mechanisms for implementation of policies. Despite this, level of implementation can be called as satisfactory. All three components of MPD-2001 contributed towards successful implementation of the proposals in following manner.

## 6.3.1 Population projections and policies

Population projections of MPD-2001 came almost close to the figures provided by the Census of India for 2001. MPD-2001 projected 12.8 million population plus 1.2 million i.e. 14 million population against the population given by the Census of 13.78 million. Due to almost accurate assessment of population, right targets were set for the various sectors like physical and social infrastructure, transport, trade, employment etc.

## 6.3.2 Population norms and space standards

Physical and social infrastructure in the form of urban extension projects i.e. Rohini Phase I, II, III, IV and V, Dwarka Phase I and II and Narela and huge housing projects like Vasant Kunj also helped to create facilities and infrastructure in the entire Delhi. In fact these urban extension projects have created a huge amount of physical and social infrastructure between existing built-up areas and rural Delhi, which used to lack in such infrastructure. A glance at above Table 6.1 shows that a large number of schools, hospitals, and road networks, employment centers and above all housing have been created. It became possible because of population norms and space standards provided by MPD-2001, and implemented by the DDA in its urban extension projects (also refer to Fig. 6.1).

## 6.3.3 Development code and monitoring

Development control mechanisms, permissibility and Land Use Plan of MPD-2001 helped to guide the physical development of the city within the overall framework of master plan policy related to population, urban extensions and desired densification, etc., within its projects.

Desire for new methods and avenues of action has given rise to more effective kind of urban planning, which would offer better control over predictable urban phenomenon in the 21st century. Let us visualize the broad lines of the new framework.

## 6.4 Broad lines of the new framework

- The master plan remains a vital document even after its critics have performed an early funeral. However master plan shall concentrate on its functions of monitoring and act as an instrument ensuring consistency between all projects and policies that are intended to have an impact on the city's future.
- The master plan has to deal with the emerging phenomenon of borderless cities. Therefore it should encompass largest possible

area which includes regional, sub-regional or metropolitan area land use plan of which it is a part.

- Master plan tends to be philosophical and theoretical document. A balance between planning postulates and mechanisms to implement its proposals should be achieved.
- Master plan needs to be made simpler for better understanding of its text and proposals.
- All the proposals related to land use, physical targets and implementation has to be presented in table format; clearly indicating concerned agency responsible for implementation of the master plan proposals.
- Planning mechanisms need to be clearly identified for monitoring, and to oversee implementation of master plan proposals. Such mechanisms may consist of a high-level committee under the chairmanship of Governor or Lt. Governor of the territory. All concerned civic bodies and government agencies are made members of such committee.
- Such high-level committee may be given statutory powers under act to issue directives to the concerned departments/agencies to carry out proposals of master plan proposals.
- Master plan must act as interface between planning, implementing agencies and decision makers.

Traditional approaches to land use planning have produced mixed results all over the world. Master plan for Delhi is no exception. On the one hand it produced serviced land for housing and networks of excellent physical and social infrastructure in its urban development projects (land acquired, developed and disposed off by the DDA). On the other hand issues related to unauthorized colonies, walled city and special area remained unaddressed.

Master plan proposals are successfully implemented where:

- Implementing agencies are clearly identified or implementing agencies are local bodies and MPD-2001 proposals have become part of annual action plan or budget of that agency.
- In most of the cases land was made available to these agencies by the DDA. For example land was allotted for hospitals, schools, fire station, police stations and sewage treatment plants and water treatment plants, etc.

Master plan proposals remained unaddressed where:

**70**
- Role of agencies was not clear and

- There was no allocation of resources in terms of land or finances. For example, polices and proposals related to the Walled City, Special Area etc.

## 6.5    Conclusions

Non-implementation of some of the Master Plan policies has created an impression that traditional land use planning has contributed to unbalanced development of cities, distortion in land and housing markets. Although it is not land use planning alone, but other factors like inappropriate policies, standards and political exigencies that have largely negated long-term planning policies. The concept of master plan stays despite many odds. Implementation mechanisms need to be added to existing policy framework. Urban planning needs to open up a new chapter in its education as well as practice. Planning must concentrate on governance, politics and process of decision making.

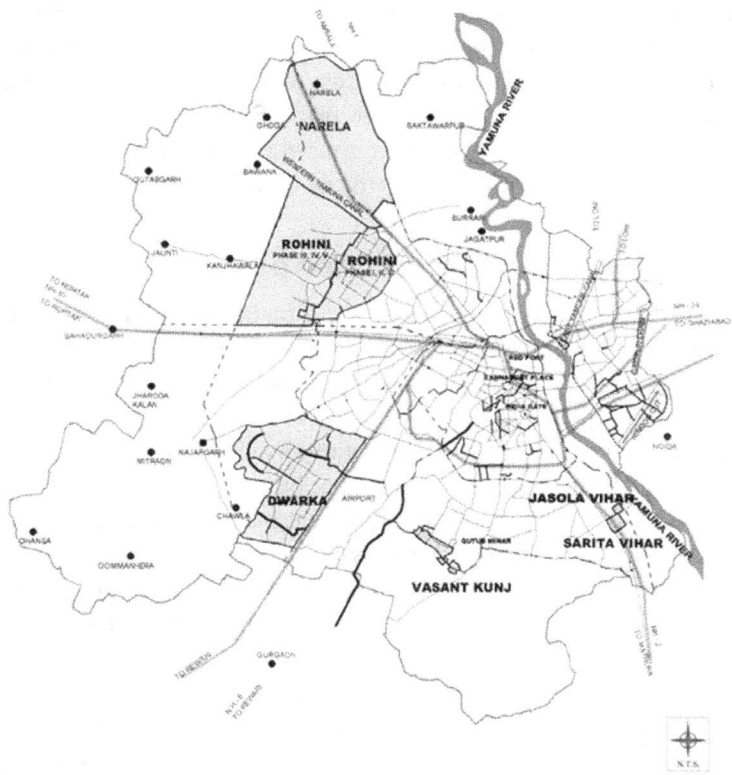

**Figure 6.1**  Major Urban Development Projects by DDA as Per MPD 2001

# Future trends in urban planning: Changing the tradition of master plan making in the Indian context

## 7.1 Introduction

Independence of India resulted in two-fold impact on towns and cities: First, sudden influx of population in the cities; and second, uncontrolled physical expansion of settlements. To deal with unprecedented growth of settlements, conscious efforts on the part of government resulted in promoting town planning legislation and development policies. One of the instruments to promote planned physical development was preparation of master plans for cities. State governments were entrusted with the task of preparation of master plans for cities through their town planning departments. During the last five decades, various state governments have prepared at least few hundred master plans. By the turn of this century, it will be interesting to look back at the whole process of master plans preparation and evaluate them in terms of their benefits.

## 7.2 Morphology of master plans

Physical planning seeks to bring about qualitative changes in human settlements, and in order to do so it must identify and concentrate on such behavioral and organizational changes, which would be necessary to ensure the plan implementation. Planning has been a continuous process of coordinated short-term actions within the framework of a guiding policy (Wakely, 1976). With rapidly changing political and economic situation, the context of operational area of physical planning is also changing. An era of e-commerce and liberalization will have definite impact on physical planning in general. Therefore planning will have to undergo a change to transform its image from a 'process of controls' to 'process of resource mobilization'.

Let us trace the brief journey of town planning. As per recorded history, town planning has existed for five thousand years. History of town planning is as old as history of human civilization. However, purpose of this chapter is not to discuss the history of town planning but to discuss evolution of master plans. History of master plans is a century old. The twentieth century saw changes in dimension and nature of urban planning. As world population exploded on the world scene, towns grew into cities and cities exploded into metropolises, adding totally new dimension to urban planning. Because of this fact, urban planning tends to touch almost all spheres of city life and address to cities dynamic problems.

Today almost all cities and metropolises of the world have town plans or master plans in one or other form. Sometimes its successive versions were called as master or structure plans, or master schemes, or extensive modifications, or extension, or regulation plans. Master plans reflected urban policies or strategies of that city or region. Evolution of urban planning is closely interlinked with scientific and industrial development. Roots of current town planning practices could be traced back to the end of 19th century. Three major periods in chronological order can be identified.

## 7.2.1    First period: End of 19th century and the first half of 20th century

This period belonged to industrialization and economic growth. It also coincided with colonization era by various world powers. Cities had moderate population growth. There were few master plans or schemes during this period. Individuals with visions designed most of these schemes and these were named after their authors. Many master plans were established for the largest cities of that time. Following are few major examples in various sub continents.

- In Europe: Oldest example is Rome (1908, Sam Just Plan), Antwerp – the Ruhr Region (1920), followed by Madrid (1910–1931), Copenhagen (1939 – Prost Plan), London (1939 – Abercrombie Plan)
- In North America: Comparable examples are Chicago (1909), Washington and New York (1929)
- In South America: Rio de Janeiro (Agache, 1928), Sao Paulo (1930)
- In Asia: Tokyo (1918–1923)

In India, in the beginning of 20$^{th}$ century Britishers started establishing Improvement Trusts in cities like Bombay, Delhi and Calcutta, etc. Improvement Trusts were empowered to prepare and implement town-planning schemes. Visit of Sir Patrick Geddes during 1915–1920 was instrumental in boosting planning activities in India. Town planning in India was greatly influenced by the Britishers. Sir Lutyen was planning the new capital of British India at New Delhi around this time.

## 7.2.2    Second period: From fifties to the seventies

This period was marked by the stark increase in population and strong economic growth. Post World War II scenario saw rise of the East and West Block and de-colonization. By this time hundreds of cities around the world were having master plan. It is difficult to list these master plans. During this period, the concept of structure plan gained popularity and was seen as successor to master plans. In India, this period recorded major event in planning activity. The master plan for Delhi was published in 1962, and Delhi Development Authority was set up for implementation of the plan. This plan proved to be the forerunner of many master plans in the country. By 1970 as many as 200 master plans were prepared for various towns and cities in India.

## 7.2.3    Third period: Last quarter of twentieth century

This period marked the stabilization of world population and major world economies. Some of the major developments during this period have been globalization of trade, major technological and scientific developments that altered and interfered with urban space in a big way. This period also saw rise of environmental concerns, which had over riding effect on master plan proposals.

In India, compared to the West, this period experienced marked shift in focus from urban planning to regional planning. This resulted in creation of Calcutta Metropolitan Development (CMDA) in 1970 and Bombay (Mumbai) Metropolitan Development Authority in 1975. For the first time, planning efforts were made to prepare regional plans for areas consisting of few administrative districts and few thousand square kilometers. These regional development authorities were empowered to implement regional plans. Most significant is the Development Plan for Calcutta Metropolitan District covering an area of about 480 sq km, which was published in 1966 with the assistance of the Ford Foundation team. Bombay Metropolitan Regional Plan was notified in 1973, which envisaged the city of New Bombay. Creation of the National Capital Region Planning Board for implementation of the National Capital Region (NCR) Plan for the region centered on the capital city of Delhi was also a major development in this direction.

Another significant development of this period was concern for environment, which resulted in enactment of many legislations on pollution control by state governments. Major event was passing of the National Environment Act, 1986 and creation of the Ministry of Environment and Forest under central government.

## 7.2.4    The twenty first century

In April 2005, the Ministry of Urban Development Government of India notified Draft Master Plan for Delhi 2021, for inviting objections and suggestions. The third Master Plan for Delhi marks a departure from earlier two master plans. Major changes are expected in decade old policy of large-scale land acquisition, monopoly in housing sector and involvement of the private sector in land assembly, etc. Some of the salient features of Master Plan for Delhi 2021 have been dealt with in latter part of this chapter. Simultaneously, almost to match with the draft MPD2021, Regional Plan 2021 was notified by the National Capital Region Board.

# 7.3    Past trends

Urban planning in former British colonies has largely depended on the British town planning methods and practices. Adoption of master plans, structure plans and local plans system by many colonial countries is almost reflection of a system adopted by England and Wales in 1968 and in Scotland sometimes later. The form and content of development plans in our country is similar to those in Britain. Even the detailed methodology of preparing structure and master plans is taken from a 'Development Plan Manual' published by the HMSO of Britain. Further, large number of town planners are trained and educated in the British institutions. In turn these town planners ensured dependence on British planning system. There was a proposal by the Department of Environment (DoE) of England and Wales for radical changes in the planning system. The British planning system has been the foundation of all master plans and structure plans preparation process in India. But this very foundation of planning system is being challenged in Britain itself. After experimenting with the system for about two decades, it became clear to the British planners that structure planning system is too cumbersome. Department of Environment of England and Wales (DoE) pointed out through a series of circulars to relax planning controls.

In this context DoE circular 22/80 asks local planning authorities to grant planning permissions for development unless there are sound and clear-cut reasons for refusals. A ministerial order further advises that structure plans should be limited to policies and general proposals of structural importance. By mid-1980s it was clear that the days of the structure plan were soon to be over. This led to the publication of a consultative Green Paper by DoE entitled 'The Future of Development Plans' in 1986 recommending major changes to urban planning system. The most radical proposal of the Green Paper was abolition of the two-tier structure plan system in urban areas. Local plans system was to be abolished and replaced with a single tier system of development planning. In other words structure planning was to be scrapped.

The consultative Green Paper stated the following main reasons for proposed changes:

- Existing planning system is very slow and cumbersome process for preparation and approval of structure plans. Preparation of approved structure plans for entire England and Wales took 14 years.
- As a result, some of policies and proposals were out of date by the time these were approved.

There are close similarities between the urban planning system of England and many developing countries including India. Radical changes in the English system are likely to have implications in India and other developing countries. This peculiar situation has put planners in dilemma: Whether to continue with the present system of planning, which is largely inherited from the British, while the basic foundation of British planning system is crumbling in the country of its origin. It appears that planning process is in a period of transition. Problems and conditions of planning are no longer the same. It is imperative to find new solutions for the challenging demands of planning beyond the conventional concepts of planning.

## 7.4 Limitations of master plans

In the present environment, role of master plan is limited; hence, also their effects. However, comprehensive, realistic and relevant it may be, a master plan alone is a sufficient force making it possible to determine the course of city's transformation over a 10–20 years period. Actual implementation is mostly dependent on the conditions, instruments and means related to urban planning. In addition, shortcomings and failures should not lead to abandoning the very principle of planning, or formulating a master plan.

New specifications could be that a master plan should form the core of a continuous urban planning process, a realistic framework for the medium and long-term development of a city, a reference giving coherence to urban development and planning decisions taken by the authorities. The plan when it is formulated and when the indispensable regular revisions are carried out should be an opportunity to take stock of the city, to analyze and understand the mechanisms involved.

## 7.5 Emerging trends in urban planning

The rigidity of master plan created restlessness among political circles. First sign of political urgency was visible in the form of Delhi Master Plan

2021 Guidelines, issued by the Ministry of Urban Development, Government of India in July 2003. Issues like regularization of unauthorized colonies including industrial clusters, informal sector, mixed land use, which were less important issues during the period of Master Plan for Delhi, 2001, took the central stage in MPD 2021. Some of the significant guidelines are as follow:

In a major departure, a suitable alternative to the past policy of large-scale acquisition and development by disposal of land by DDA was to be put in place.

- *Mixed land use:* Allowing shops in residential, commercial and office use of industrial premises and regularization of concentration of industries to the extent of 70 percent or more in some non-industrial areas.
- *Involvement of private sector in housing*
- *Regularization unauthorized colonies*
- Master Plan, 2021 to include perspective plans prepared by relevant agencies as an annexure.

In the light of the above, a draft of the Master Plan for Delhi 2021 has been notified with the following innovative features.

- First time, section of Review of Past Experience is introduced as a part of 'Vision' under the introduction chapter. It includes review of the first two master plans that is MPD 1962 and MPD 2001 and review of the scheme of large-scale land acquisition and its relevance in the present context, involvement private developers in housing sector and assembly of land, etc.
- Plan review and monitoring aspect has been further detailed out in groups for follow-up planning and integrated implementation of the plan. There are 10 proposed groups to take care of various aspects like infrastructure, enhancement, spatial data infrastructure, legal framework review groups. Periodic reviews are proposed to ensure mid-term corrections and modifications if needed in the master plan policies.
- Master Plan for Delhi 2021 includes perspective plan for development of infrastructure, which is prepared with the involvement of the relevant agencies and experts.
- Land use plan also simplifies number of land uses, hierarchy of land uses and total omission of rural land use from the land use plan, and replace by new category 'urbanizable area', and sports has been treated at par with social infrastructure and not green or recreational category.

- Transportation aspect strives for modern multimodal network of roads, rail, metro rail, etc., with underground road and tube roads, elevated roads, etc.; at the same time very simple but effective concept of 'urban relief road' has been introduced for the first time.
- Environment and ecology gets special attention.
- Local area plans, as micro-level planning instrument, have been introduced to suit municipal ward level area.

## 7.6     Conclusion

Up till now, planning has been a technocratic process using master plans as a tool for identification of problems, analysis and decision making, working almost in isolation from the major stakeholders.

Planners are not fully aware of political milieu surrounding them. It is high time planners realize that political urgency at times works at cross purposes of long-term planning which often negate long-term goals. These have implications for the approaches to planning which are appropriate.

Improvement to data, technologies and techniques will not obtain initial support and resource, unless they can be shown to contribute to the tasks that matter politically. Political legitimacy is in turn an essential condition of effective urban planning and management.

Situation raises a question, whether to devote resources to improve the quality of urban spatial plans or urban managers should concentrate on governance. A number of key realizations underpinned the approach to the planning.

- Urban planning should be responsive and not perspective.
- 'People-First' planning approach.
- Orientation of planning should be to reduce poverty rather than to achieve a particular city form.
- Must recognize importance of market forces and its capability to create innovation that cannot be anticipated because preference changes over time.
- They must concentrate on governance, politics, and process of decision-making. Without it, spatial development plans are unlikely to be useful like in the past.

## References

- Government of India (1981). *Master Plan for Delhi, 2001*, Government of India, New Delhi.

- Government of India (2005). *Master Plan for Delhi, 2021*, Government of India, New Delhi.

- ISOCARP (2000). Millennium Report Findings for the Future – The work of the Congresses of ISoCaRP 1965–1999, ISOCARP, The Hague.

- Jain, A.K. (2005). Master Plan for Delhi-2021-Making a Difference, AMDA Conference at Abu, Rajasthan.

- LES CAHIERS – DE L'INSTITUT D'AMENAGEMENT, ET D'URBANISME, DELA REGION D'ILE DE FRANCE 'Plantification Urbaine?' REPONSES DE METROPOLES Quarterly Review, AOUT 1993.

- Rakodi, C. (2001). Forget Planning, Put Politics First? Priorities for urban management in developing countries, ITC Journal Issue 3.

- UNDP (1994). Monograph on the International Regional Exchange and Transfer of Effective Practice on Urban Management, Manila.

# 8

# Role of water in stabilizing cities: Case of Delhi city

## 8.1    Introduction

Ancient Vedas have described the role of Divine, Panacean and Emancipative Water in

Vedic Religion in following manner:

"yāpo divyyā uta vyā sravanti khanitrimyā utyā vyā yaḥ svayañjyāḥ\
samudrārthā yāh śucayah pāvakās tā āpo devTrīha māmavantu \\"

*(Waters which come from heaven, or those that wander dug from the earth, or flowing free by nature, bright, purifying, speeding to the Ocean, here let those Waters, Goddesses, protect me.)*

Water has played important role in evolution of human civilization. Water, being fused with ancient Indian ethos, as we learn from the time-honoured literature, was highly revered for its unparalleled prowess and multiform presence and taken to be more than an essential need for all forms of life both in this very life and the hereafter. Beyond the horizons of our current knowledge of water which relies completely upon scientific underpinning, the honours received by water in Vedic religion solemnly fill us with owe and insist that we ponder over our mechanic wheel of life rushing towards an increasingly chaotic tomorrow.

Half of humanity is living in cities, and within two decades, nearly 60 per cent of the world's people will be living in cities. Urban growth is most rapid in the developing world, where cities gain an average of 0.5 million residents every month. The exploding urban population growth creates unprecedented challenges, among which provision for water for sustaining urban population is most pressing and essential.

Two main challenges related to water are affecting the sustainability of human urban settlements: the lack of access to safe water and, and increasing water-related disasters such as floods and droughts. These problems have enormous consequences on the environment, economic growth and development. Water has been most important stabilizing factor throughout the history of human civilization.

Following is an overview :

## (a) Ancient times

Water has been most important natural resource for flourishing of not only citied but also human civilization. Historical cities of Mohenjo-Daro and Harappa flourished on the bank of river Indus for centuries due to availability of water and fertile land. As historians/ archaeologists point out from ruins of these cities, a change in the course of river or flooding caused end of the cities and great civilization.

**Figure 8.1** Ancient City of Mohenjo-Daro

## (b) Historical times

Fatehpur Sikri is a historic city in North India which is a mere ghost town today. Mughal emperor of India 'Akbar' had visited a saint known as Salim Chishti who then foretold that the emperor would have a second son who will survive to become a great ruler. When in 1569 a second son was indeed born to Akbar, he decided to move his capital from Agra to Sikri in honour of the saint Salim and started the construction of an architectural wonder of a town. It was then located around a natural water body lake around which evidences of civilization can be found. This place was abandoned then due to scarcity of water which could not support the growing population.

**Figure 8.2** Historical City: Fatehpur Sikri (India)

Water is the single most essential component of the physical infrastructure for improved quality of life. Urban Water Sector is a zone of serious mismanagement. Increased urbanization, population growth and living standards have been major drivers in the increase of urban water use in the past century. The amount of urban water use depends on climate, level and efficiency of public supply services, patterns and habits of water use by the population, technological changes (for example, water saving technologies and use of alternative sources) and socioeconomic instruments.

Most urban areas have depleted, polluted or destroyed their local sources of water like rivers, lakes and tanks and in many cases even groundwater. The rainfall is generally seen as a bane rather than boon as it brings floods because the drainage systems are seriously ill designed or mismanaged. Lack of provision of adequate minimum water for vast proportions of poorer segments on the one hand and wasteful use without paying even cost prices by more prosperous segments on the other hand is typical picture of most urban areas.

## 8.2    Existing scenario of water supply in Delhi

As per Master Plan of Delhi -2021, the present water demand for potable water in Delhi has been assessed as 990 Million Gallon per day (MGD) @ 60 Gallon per capita per day (GPCD) for all uses. No allowance is made for use of potable water for parks & lawns / horticulture/agriculture purposes due to water shortage. The Delhi Jal Board anticipates that by the year 2021 about 1380 MGD potable water @ 60 GPCD for a population of 230 lacs shall be required. However, the DDA has projected the 2021 water demand as 1840 MGD @ 80 GPCD.

The total city requirement is considered as 80 GPCD out of which 50 GPCD is for domestic requirement and 30 GPCD for non-domestic purposes. The domestic water requirements of 50 GPCD comprises of 30 GPCD for potable needs and 20 GPCD for non-potable water. The requirement of potable water out of total requirement of 80 GPCD has been assessed as 35 GPCD (30 GPCD for domestic and 5 GPCD for non-domestic demand) while the demand for non-potable water has been assessed as 45 GPCD i.e. 20 GPCD for domestic and 25 GPCD for non-domestic purposes.

Delhi mainly receives its water from the following 3 sources:

- Surface Water: 86% of Delhi's total water supply comes from surface water, namely the Yamuna River, which equals 4.6% of this resource through interstate agreements.

- Sub-surface water: Rainey wells and Tubewells. This source, which is met though rainfall (approx. 611.8 mm in 27 rainy days), and unutilized rainwater runoff, is 193 MCM (million cubic meters).
- Graduated Resources: It is estimated at 292 MCM, however current withdrawal equals 312 MCM.

According to various estimates, a proportion of 50% of Delhi's population lives in some kind of informal, unplanned and/or precarious settlement. Among them, more than two million people, representing more than 15% of the total population, live in illegal squatter settlements and face a permanent risk of eviction. The accountability of the municipal utility in charge of water supply and sanitation towards populations living in informal settlements is loosely defined, and most of them do not have a proper connection to the network. According to the Water and Sanitation Program (WSP), more than 40% of the urban poor in India rely only on groundwater resources through hand pumps and shallow wells for their water supply.

Around 75% of the households in Delhi are reported to have access to piped municipal supply either through a private connection or a common stand point, and around 20% of the population relies on hand pumps tapping the shallow aquifer for heir water supply. The contribution of groundwater to the municipal supply is around 11% in terms of volume, which represents around 370 Million a Day (MLD). This figure is often used as an indicator of the relative importance of groundwater for the city's water supply.

## 8.3 Problems of water supply in Delhi

The position of Delhi both as the centre of an urban agglomeration and as an independent state impacts significantly on its access to water resources. Water is a state subject as per the constitution of India. As a consequence, both water supply and water resources management fall under the responsibilities of state governments. In the National Capital Territory (NCT), the public utility in charge of water supply and sanitation - the Delhi Jal Board (DJB) - acts as an independent agency under the authority of the state government.

However, given the small size of the NCT, the DJB relies heavily on surface resources which are mobilized outside the NCT. Since 2005, the Delhi Jal Board received approximately 1 million m3/day from the Bhakra dam fed by tributaries of the Indus, another million m3/day from the Yamuna, around 0.45 million m3/day from the Upper Ganga Canal, and around 0.38 million m3/day were obtained through exploitation of the local groundwater resources. Its right to those resources depends on several interstate agreements and their application by other states, namely Haryana and Punjab as far as waters from the Indus tributaries are concerned and Uttar Pradesh and Uttaranchal as far as Ganga river waters are concerned.

There are several problems and issues related to water supply and distribution in Delhi which are as follows:

### (a) Disparity in supply

Besides overall city level shortfall in water supply, there are wide disparities in the availability of water various parts of the city. Non-availability of even minimum supply of 135 LPCD (as per MPD 2001) to a significant proportion of city's population living in marginal settlements is the real concern. Lack of assured and timely supply of water at low pressure and quality standard not being maintained are other routine complaints of many colonies in the city.

### (b) Unaccounted for water

There are significantly high losses (nearly 30%) in the entire water supply system at different stages of raw water transmission, distribution network and other pilferage's/ unauthorized tapping.

### (c) Lack of inter-agency co-ordination:

Although Delhi Jal Board is the nodal agency for water at the city level; the issues related to land /land use and development controls are with Delhi Development Authority, NDMC, Cantonment Board, CPWD, Railways and other local bodies, who procure bulk quantity and maintain / manage the distribution network within the areas under their jurisdiction. Absence of a synchronized annual five-year programme of each agency in line with well laid down overall city development programme set out in Master Plan for Delhi, and scientific monitoring system of executing the schemes is lacking. It results in delays and system inefficiencies besides additional expenditure due to cost and time over runs.

### (d) Dependence on the sources outside Delhi

The major source to meet the raw water requirement of Delhi has been though inter-state allocations of Yamuna water and in future through prepared storage dams to be developed in Himachal Pradesh, Uttar Pradesh, etc. Most of these long - term projects are behind schedule and may take at least 10 years or more for a definite commitment about the assured quality of water to Delhi. The carrier canal and treatment plant, etc. for the same are also to be finalized both within / outside Delhi. However, there has been a lack of emphasis on recharge of ground water and of schemes to harness the source / potential of water in Delhi which are necessary for sustainable development.

### (e) Local groundwater and its non-management

Although ground water abstraction is in theory regulated in Delhi. The authorities in charge of the enforcement of the regulation do not have the practical means of controlling private abstraction. In practice, abstraction is tolerated as a compensation for the failure of the public supply systems. As a consequence, water table is falling at an increasing pace in several areas of NCT Delhi. The southern and western of Delhi, where piped supply does not match the growing residential demand are the most severely affected area. In the Chattarpur alluvial basin, were the water tables are falling at the highest rate, as well as in the western part of the state were recent urbanization is taking place in areas affected by the occurrence of saline water at shallow depths, the availability of fresh water will come to an end in a few years if abstraction continues at current rate. In addition to this, Delhi's groundwater resources are subject to various forms of pollution.

### (f) Over dependence on planned funds

There has been a widening gap in the balance sheets (revenue & expenditure) of the Delhi Jal Board. Low tariffs, ineffective billing and collection of dues, and operation/maintenance inefficiencies attribute to the bad financial health of DJB. Principles of water demand management; privatization and involvement of NGOs and CBOs at different stages of water system and sound management tools/techniques are relatively missing.

### (g) Areas lacking adequate focus

- Phased augmentation/replacement of distribution network in the congested central city/urban villages etc.
- Public awareness and media coverage for minimizing wastages of water.
- Effective implementation of legislation to curb the extraction of ground water.

## 8.4    Water management in Delhi

Water management is the activity of planning, developing, distribution, managing and optimum use of water resources under defined water policies and regulations. In context of NCT of Delhi, it includes the following:

### 8.4.1 Management of water resources & water treatment

(a) Integrated approach for water resource management: the six drainage basins to be made self-sustainable in water requirement by integrating water-sewerage-drainage systems.

(b) Recycling of treated waste water (bod 30 mg/l) for horticulture, irrigation, industries, construction, fire etc. by

- Mandatory ecoparks with dual pipe system at all STP's
- Treated recycled water from STP's (350 mgd)
- Treated effluent from CETP'S

(c) Delhi Jal Board with the help of specialized agencies experts, NGOs, etc., should take up preparation of a detailed plan for water augmentation potential of Delhi. This may include:

- Water mapping by
  i. Identification of traditional water structures on land-use plan and schemes to revive them e.g. baolis, historic reservoirs, ponds, etc.
  ii. Utilization of abandoned quarry pits for water storage and augmentation of existing lakes / depressions for additional storage of rain / flood water
  iii. On- channel storage and recharge of water in trunk storm water drains, iv) Selection of areas within the river bed to be identified for water ponds and the concept of rain water harvesting for ground water re-charge are to be suitably emphasized.

- Possibility of the re-cycling of wastewater, legislation to minimize extraction of ground water within the specific limits, and measures to conserve water.

- Traditional water -harvesting model.

- Runoff is harvested through tanks, supported by his yielding wells and structures like baories, kundis and water holes.

### 8.4.2 Management of the ground water table

The ground water resources of 7 districts of NCT, Delhi are over-exploited with stage of development reaching to even 24% in south district. Moreover, the presence of saline aquifers below a depth of 30 to 40 m further limits the development of ground water resources. Thus the complex ground water regime of NCT, Delhi needs scientific planning to make the ground water resources as sustainable supplement source of water supply in NCT, Delhi. The groundwater management strategy in NCT Delhi should emphasize on the limited development of potential aquifers' of Delhi and augmentation to the groundwater resources of Delhi by rainwater harvesting and artificial recharge to the groundwater.

**Figure 8.3** Traditional water-harvesting model: Runoff is harvested through tanks, supported by high yielding wells and structures like baories, kundies and water holes

**Figure 8.4** Trapping of Runoff: Figures above shows Channels and gullies are created to direct excess rain water into open wells and the water collects in the well. This water then percolates into the ground and within a week 3,00,000 litres of water percolates 100 ft. below ground level to recharge the ground water bodies.

The rapidly declining water level of Delhi is attributed mainly due to rampant urbanization and enhanced groundwater withdrawal and reduction in the available open space for recharge to groundwater. The **87** situation can be improved by adopting rainwater harvesting and artificial recharge to ground water measures. The Master Plan for rainwater harvesting and artificial recharge of NCT Delhi estimated that nearly 440 MCM of rainwater can be harvested annually in Delhi and utilized for artificial recharge to groundwater. The artificial recharge to groundwater can be taken up by adopting different measures like rainwater harvesting at the level of individuals, at the level of colonies and by the institutions.

The Central Groundwater Board of NCT Delhi has taken up the leadership of spearheading rain water harvesting in NCT Delhi. The rainwater harvesting effort by CGWB in JNU and NT campuses resulted in to rise in water level to the tune of about 2 to 3 metre in vicinity of the area where the project was implemented. Similar rainwater harvesting effort in President Estate resulted in the rise of water level in the range of 1 to 4 meters in the vicinity of the areas where the project was implemented.

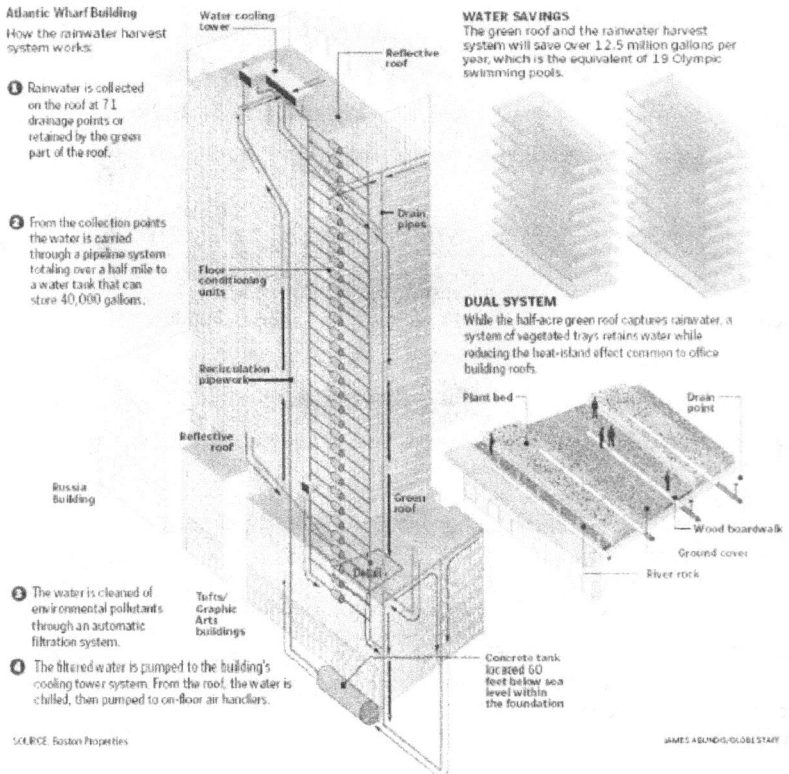

**Figure 8.5** Roof-top rain water harvesting in a multipurpose building (containing office, residential, retail and public spaces) and various other measures adopted for water saving & reuse of waste water. (*Source*: Boston Properties: James Abundis/Globe Staff)

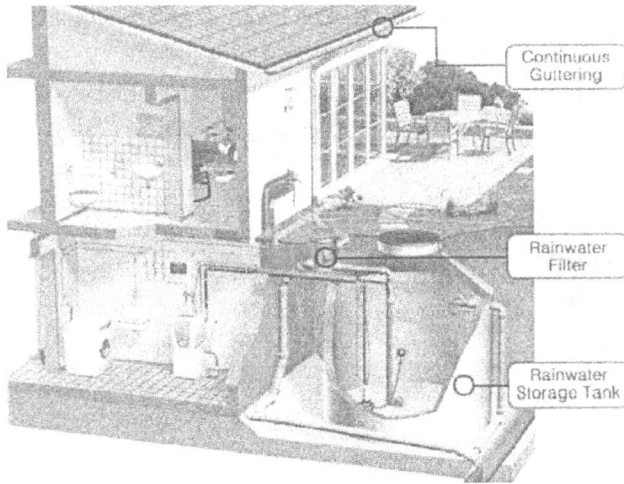

**Figure 8.6** The details of rain water harvesting in plotted housing development and its reuse. (*Source*: Boston Properties: James Abundis/Globe Staff)

## 8.5 Conclusion

In order to understand the interaction between the co-existing approaches to the problem of water supply, one has to take into account the time frame of the different dynamics at stake. Several factors will affect the evolution of the current system towards one of the scenarios described here. Among them, we can mention:

- The political process of interstate surface water allocation, which will determine the ability of Delhi to increase the volume of raw water available for its centralized system.
- The ability of the municipal utility to improve its efficiency and to manage the demand in a short period of time.
- The institutional integration between service management and local resources development.
- The evolution of technologies for aquifer recharge and recovery, and decentralized wastewater reclamation.
- The involvement of communities in the conception and the management of alternative systems.

## References

- Augustin, Maria (2008), "The role of groundwater in Delhi's water supply", CERNA - Centre d'economie indusrielle, Paris, France

- Seneviratne, Rohana, Divine, Panacean and Emancipative Water in Vedic Religion, University of Oxford
- Master Plan for Delhi 2021 (notified on 7th February 2007)
- Work Studies Report of Sub Groups for MPD 2021, MPPR Unit, DDA.
- www. rainwaterharavesting. org.
- www.indiaenvironmentportal.org.in

# Monitoring and mapping of urban sprawl Delhi, 1988

## LIST OF MAPS

1. Location map of Delhi
2. Union Territory of Delhi
3. Seven cities of Delhi
4. Population of Delhi (in 1981 and 2001)
5. Urban sprawl of Delhi (in 1975–1987)
6. Land use / land cover map, Delhi
7. Direction of growth
8. Interpretation keys – TM
9. Delhi Scene, 1987

## 9.1    Introduction

Extraordinary population growth and rapid changes in population distribution are two of the most important phenomena associated with urban growth. The rapid urbanization process and the concentration of population in metropolitan areas is a result of the mass migration of people from rural to urban areas. This rapid growth in metropolitan areas has resulted in number of problems. In spite of the increase in per capita income and personal income, the condition of urban areas is worsening. Though the supply of goods and services has vastly increased, the quality of life has deteriorated. The rapid influx of migrants into central cities has resulted in overcrowding. Meanwhile, the movement of middle class residents to the outlying suburbs has created the *urban sprawl*.

Land use is one of the essential factors influencing the pattern of urban development. The limited space within the city combined with the growing space requirements for different purposes outlines the framework of land uses and creates demand for it.

Over the years, rapid technological changes are influencing urban growth and it is out pacing the slow planning process. This results in a contraction between planning and reality.

### 9.1.1    Why monitoring?

Fast technological changes coupled with rapid population growth are having devastating effect on the urban areas. Large number of slums and squatters' colonies are dotting city scene. Problem is more aggrieved by lack of detection mechanism.

Urban planning has to depend on information system for planning purpose and decision-making. Need for such urban information system and monitoring framework is long felt. Monitoring will help

(i)   detect changes in urban areas, and

(ii)  update of base maps, which forms basis for all planning work.

Momentum of the urban development has outpaced the traditional techniques of survey. At this juncture, remote sensing techniques have stepped into scene to fill up the gap.

## 9.2    The monitoring

In the beginning of this decade, necessity of the monitoring as a built-in provision of the urban planning process was felt by the planners. The monitoring would provide sufficient technical data to anticipate changes in socio-economic fabric of the city and amend plans as required. Monitoring would also provide an opportunity to consider other aspects arising out of emerging socio-economic and physical forces. The monitoring will help to find out deficiency or gap between demand and supply. It will also act as a balancing factor between demand and supply.

'Master Plan for Delhi, Perspective 2001' is the first document to have built-in provision for monitoring. It has described the objectives of monitoring as follows:

(i)   The socio-economic and functional efficiency of the performance of human settlement has to be monitored and evaluated, so that changes required to improve the quality of life could be identified and put into action through appropriate measures.

(ii)  Any (master) plan should be continuously made responsive to the emerging socio-economic forces.

To achieve above objectives, there should be monitoring system in the plan implementation framework. There is a possibility of arresting the unintended developments taking place in the city through effective monitoring.

## 9.3    Remote sensing and monitoring

Once need for monitoring was established, a search for an appropriate technology ended with remote sensing techniques. Monitoring requires reliable data at regular time intervals. Remote sensing has capability to provide reliable and all season data at regular time interval. In case of remote sensing data products, time required for acquisition is less than manual/conventional techniques.

Remote sensing has been recognized worldwide as an effective technology for the monitoring urban and environment changes, as such data are available on repetitive basis. Specifically, aerial photographs and satellite imageries have provided to be very useful for urban planners, as they can provide basic data input on:

(i) *Urban growth* – Time series data are very useful for study of growth and its trend over the years.

ii) *Slums/encroachments* – One of the major problems faced by cities is unintended growth of slums or encroachments by squatters on public land. To an extent, this can be detected well in time.

iii) *Change detection* – It helps in updating base maps. Comparison between old base map and updated base map helps in detecting change in land uses.

(iv) *Inventory of environment* – Urban area and its environment is a fast changing scene. Development inflicts the unalterable changes on surrounding environment. Study of imageries taken over the years helps to detect the changes taken plan in surrounding environment.

(v) *Cost and time* – Compared to other remote sensing products, satellite data is cost and time effective.

## 9.4 Objectives

For urban planner, land use plan is an important tool to guide the development of the city and formulate the strategy and future.

Objective of the study is to orient trainees in the use of remote sensing data products, particularly, satellite data products. In near future, availability of satellite data products would be easier in terms of acquisition and accessibility.

Objective is to impart an ability among urban planners/users to understand the limitations of remote sensing data products from urban planning point of view. The satellite imagery is inferior, compared to aerial photographs in terms of its spatial resolution and details. This exercise will provide an opportunity to learn, what can be delineated, mapped and interpreted from satellite imagery for urban planning purpose.

However, broad objectives can be spelled as below:

(1) Monitoring of the urban sprawl of Delhi city and its urban agglomeration on 1:50,000 scale. A map has to be prepared showing

urban sprawl of Delhi at various years using multi-date land sat, MSS and TM date products.

(2) Delineating various land uses from TM on 1:50,000 scale for Delhi City, a land cover / land use map has to be prepared.

(3) Preparing a land use classification, which is compatible to the existing land use map, based on the physical characteristics of the terrain.

## 9.5    Material used

(1) Land sat MSS (FCC) diapositives of Delhi

(2) Land sat 5, TM scene of Delhi and its environs at 1:50,000 scale dated 3rd March, 1987

(3) Topographical maps of Delhi and Uttar Pradesh at 1:50,000 scale (1974)

(4) Guide map of Delhi at 1:25,000 scale (1982)

## 9.6    Instruments used

(1) Large Format Optical Enlarger

(2) KARGL Reflecting Projector

(3) Digital Planimeter

(4) Simple Light Table

## 9.7    Scope of the study

TM scene at the scale of 1:50,000 covers Delhi and its neighboring states, as it gives useful information related to vegetation, water bodies, etc., because of FCC, following studies are possible.

(1) Natural resources like forestry, water bodies, rocky lands, etc., can be easily identified and delineated.

(2) Identification of built-up areas and non-built up areas. Because of tonal variation, densities of the areas can be identified.

(3) Large green areas / parks / stadium / gold course within the built-up areas can be identified because of its peculiar colour, pattern and shape.

(4) There is possibility of identifying water-logged areas, as water and vegetation is easily identifiable on TM.

(5) By comparing this map, with existing land use map, deviations in planned development and a real growth can be tabulated.

## 9.8     Limitations

- Identification of linear features is difficult without the help of guide map and local knowledge.
- Field checking of interpreted land uses was limited to sample polygons and 132 sample points, designated on a 77 × 82 square centimeter base map at 1:50,000 scale.
- Urban sprawl does not follow the administrative boundary of the city/state.
- Interpretation of satellite imagery is much different from the interpretation of aerial photographs. In aerial photographs, shape and size of the object is recorded in proportion to the real size of the object. In satellite imagery, image largely depends on spectral response from the object. Therefore, it may not image true shape and size of the object. This leads to the misinterpretation of objects at times.

## 9.9     Study area

Delhi, the capital city of India is the study area. For urban purpose, urban agglomeration of Delhi known as 'Delhi Metropolitan Area (DMA)' is considered. DMA includes some part of Uttar Pradesh and Haryana in addition to UT of Delhi (Fig. 9.1). For land cover/land use mapping, only urban Delhi has been considered.

(i)   Delhi is situated on 280 24'17" N to 280 53'00" N latitude and 760 50'24" E to 70 20'37" E longitude (Fig. 9.1).

(ii)   Extreme greatest length – 52.90 km

(iii)   Greatest width – 48.48 km

(iv)   Area (in 1981)
- Total – 1483 sq km
- Urban – 591.9 sq km
- Rural – 891.1 sq km

(v)   Total population (in 1981) – 6220406 persons

(vi)   Density of population per sq km (UT) – 4194 per sq km

(vii)   Rainfall – Average normal rainfall for Delhi is 660 mm. In 1985, total rainfall of 857.9 mm was recorded. In 1986, total rainfall was somewhat reduced (469.4 mm).

(viii)   Temperature in Delhi varies from season to season. Average maximum temperature varies between 20°C in January to 40°C in May. Average minimum temperature varies between 8°C in January to 28°C in June.

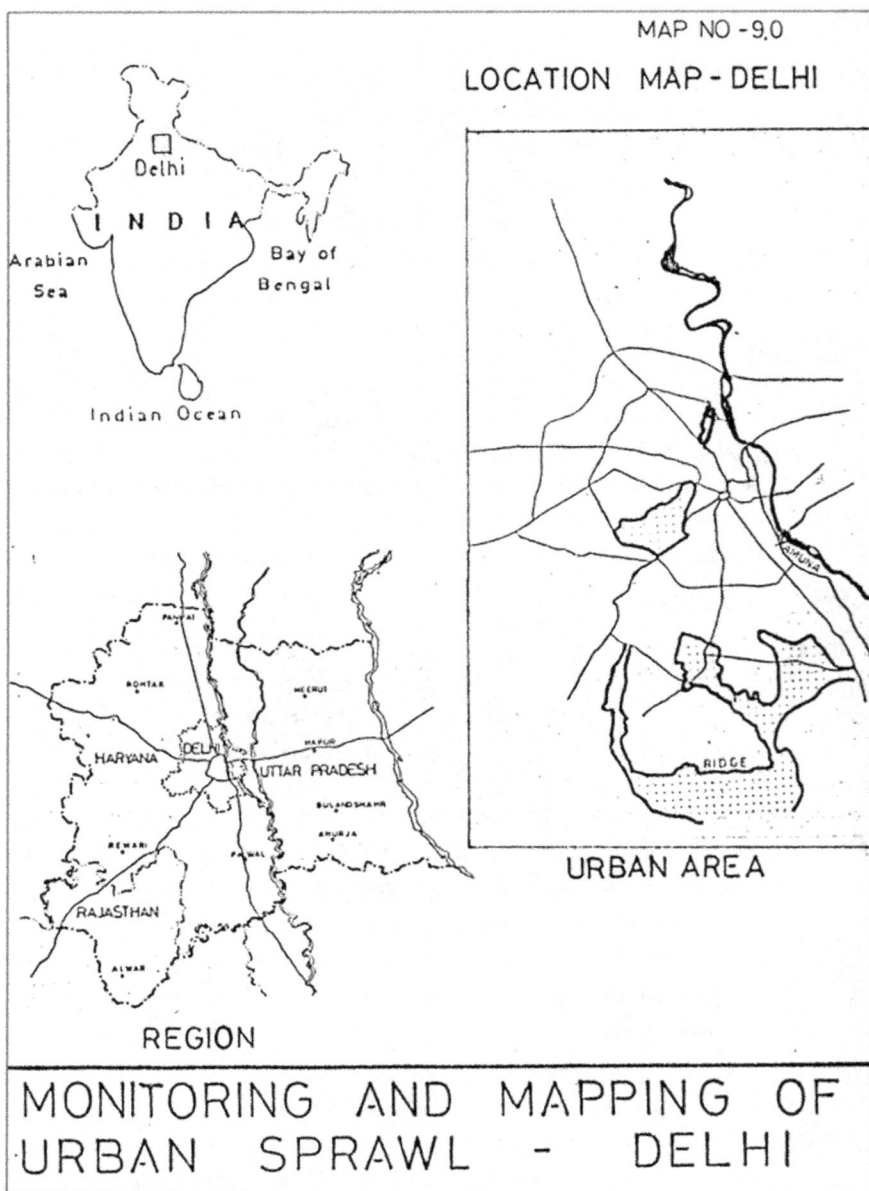

MAP NO - 9.0

LOCATION MAP - DELHI

INDIA

Delhi

Arabian Sea

Bay of Bengal

Indian Ocean

YAMUNA

RIDGE

URBAN AREA

PANIPAT

ROHTAK

MEERUT

HARYANA

DELHI

MAPUR

UTTAR PRADESH

BULANDSHAHR

REWARI

ANUPSHA

FARWAL

RAJASTHAN

ALWAR

REGION

MONITORING AND MAPPING OF
URBAN SPRAWL - DELHI

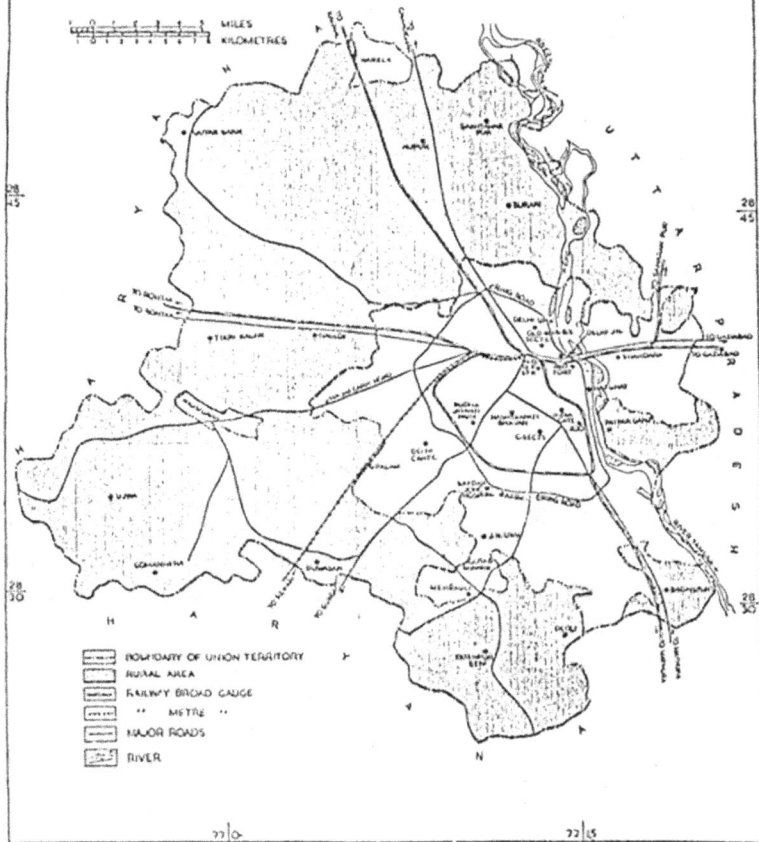

MONITORING AND MAPPING OF
URBAN SPRAWL - DELHI

## 9.10    Delhi: The evolution of the town

The origin of the Delhi is lost in antiquity. Its unique situation vis-à-vis the sub-continent has inevitably embroiled in its conquest for control. Delhi occupies a site which has been the repeatedly focus of invasion.

### 9.10.1    Location

Early settlements as tradition indicates were established on only one, usually the right bank of the river. It is a holy site; the other left side is thought to be ill-omened. There is substantial evidence that the course of Yamuna River has shifted generally in an eastward direction to its present position, where its subsequent migration is precluded by earth bundhs. The urgency of being near a water supply has influenced site selection throughout the history.

### 9.10.2    Seven cities of Delhi

The earliest settlement that originated in Delhi is traceable on the 10th century BC to the epic period of Mahabharata. It is believed that the Pandavas founded the city of Indraprastha, somewhere between the historic *Purana Quila* (The Old Fort) and Humayun's Tomb. The settlement was there for some three thousand years. It was described as well-laid roads, palatial buildings, with charming gardens and lakes. The past of the city remains shrouded in the darkness until about 11th century BC when Raja Dillu of the Mauryan dynasty founded a new city near the site where the Qutab Minar stands today. It is believed that he named the city after his own name and hence called as Dillu–Dilli–Delhi and Delhi.

It is said that in the middle of the 11th century, a Rajput king Anagpal founded another city 'Surajkund' on the old ruins of the city founded by Raja Dillu. Even in its present state of despair, it suggests the beauty it may once have possessed.

Prithviraj Chauhan's city, Lalkot and Killa Rai Pithora are regarded as the first capital city Delhi. They were also destined to be the last Hindu cities until modern times. This settlement near Qutab flourished as the centre of Hindu Empire, till the end of 12th century. With the defeat of Prithviraj Chauhan, Delhi passed on to the hands of Muslim invaders. Up to 16th century, various sultans ruled Delhi and developed their capitals at several places in the vicinity of Qutab Minar. The settlement was later incorporated in larger constellation and connected to Siri. With the advent of the Delhi Sultanate rule of non-indigenous, people prevailed through the slave of Mamulak dynasty and Khilji dynasty. The Delhi sultanate period gradually developed the base for long history. Qutub-ud-din Aibak, the founder of the slave dynasty, established his capital towards the end of 12th century on the same site where the Rajput kings ruled.

Siri, the second city, the ruling seat for another sultan is credited with digging the well-known tank at Hauz Khas on the border of which a later ruler constructed a university. This city stood further northeast of Qutab Minar.

When Tughlaq dynasty seized power, the founder king Mohmad Tughlaq build his new capital in 1320 AD, five miles east of old city and gave it a name Tughlaqabad – identified as third capital city. The new city has to be abandoned partly, as a result of a curse placed by nearby saint whose workmen were drafted to construct the city and partly because of non-availability of drinking water.

The seat of the government was therefore moved back to the old city of Qutab Minar by the successor of Tughlaq and gave it a name Jahanpanah. Translated as world's refuge, fourth city of Delhi involved a particular interesting situation. Suburbs are by no means a recent innovation, for outside the walls and attached to the ruling centre, for one reason or another, settlements have always appeared and frequently been enclosed by the extension of existing walls. The builder of Jahanpanah built his wall 'to enclose all the suburbs that had sprung up between Chauhans' Delhi and Siri'.

The last Tughlaq ruler Firoz Shah Tughlaq, however, abandoned the site and moved his capital further north near the site of Indraprastha (present day Firoz Shah Kotla ground) The area of this city, the fifth capital city of Delhi, was large; it occupied all the ground from old Indraprastha to the ridge including the site of Shahjahanabad which came in the existing much later. It was at this time when Yamuna canal with a branch to Firozabad opened up. The great Hauz Khas tank was brought into its highest development including an establishment of a university on its shores. The Indian Institute of Technology incidentally also stands today around the same site.

Dinpanah – the sixth city was on the site of older Indraprastha; it had nine miles circumference and extended from site now occupied by Humayun's Tomb to the site of Firozshah Kotla ground.

Delhi's importance was regained when Shahjahan the fifth Mughal ruler undertook the construction of an altogether new capital north of Firozshah in 1639 A.D. The completion of the seventh city took over nine years. Now popularly known as Purani Delhi, this city was built on the banks of Yamuna and was named as Shahjahanabad. This magnificent city was built with wide streets and paths and occupied the territory by the river to the north of Indraprastha of Pandavas. A wall having a circumference of about four miles was built around. The river Yamuna gave the city a perennial supply of water for drinking purpose and other needs of community. The raised plateau on the right bank of the river gave an ideal situation for the capital free from floods and at the same time having protection on the west from the possible invaders.

### 9.10.3    Civil Lines in Delhi

British arrived in 1803 under General Lake. The population was estimated to be only around 15000. The East India Company controlled the area till 1857. After the Mutiny – the Sepoy Rebellion in 1857 – the power of India was transferred from the East India Co. to the British crown in 1858.

Delhi started growing after 1857. At the historic Delhi Durbar in 1911, the King George V announced the shifting of the Capital of British India from Calcutta to Delhi. Following this announcement, a secretariat (now known as Old Secretariat) was built at Civil Lines.

### 9.10.4    Delhi: The new imperial capital

Along with the proclamation made by King George V, it was also announced that an entirely new city would be built as the capital of British India. The British Government appointed a committee of architects, headed by Sir Edwin Lutyens to plan the new capital.

Committee suggested the new site on eastern slopes of the hills to the south of Delhi. The Viceroy's Palace or Rashtrapati Bhavan was located on top of Raisina Hill and as a focal point of British Delhi. Thus, it became the eighth city in chronological order and a beginning of the present metropolitan city.

## 9.11    Urbanisation and the growth

Urbanization is a worldwide phenomenon, and the 20th century is known as a century of urbanization. The expected growth of the world population from the present 4 billion to 6 billion in the year 2000, combined with a doubling of urban population from 1.5 billion to 3 billion during the same period, poses a serious challenge to decision makers and urban scientists. The prospect of a population of 10 billion in the year 2050 makes the efficient use of land essential for the future. The unplanned development of urban regions leads to unnecessary land consumption and the destruction of good agriculture land.

In this unparalleled phenomenon of urbanization, India will not be an exception. In 1981, 156 million people were residing in urban areas. India had fourth largest concentration of urban population, after the United States, USSR and China.

One-fourth of the population of India lives in urban areas. The urban population has increased more than two and a half times over the last three decades ending 1981, registering an increase of 6 percent points from 17.3% in 1951 to 23.3% in 1981. Since the beginning of the century, the highest growth rate of urban population has been during the decade 1971–81.

MAP NO-10.1

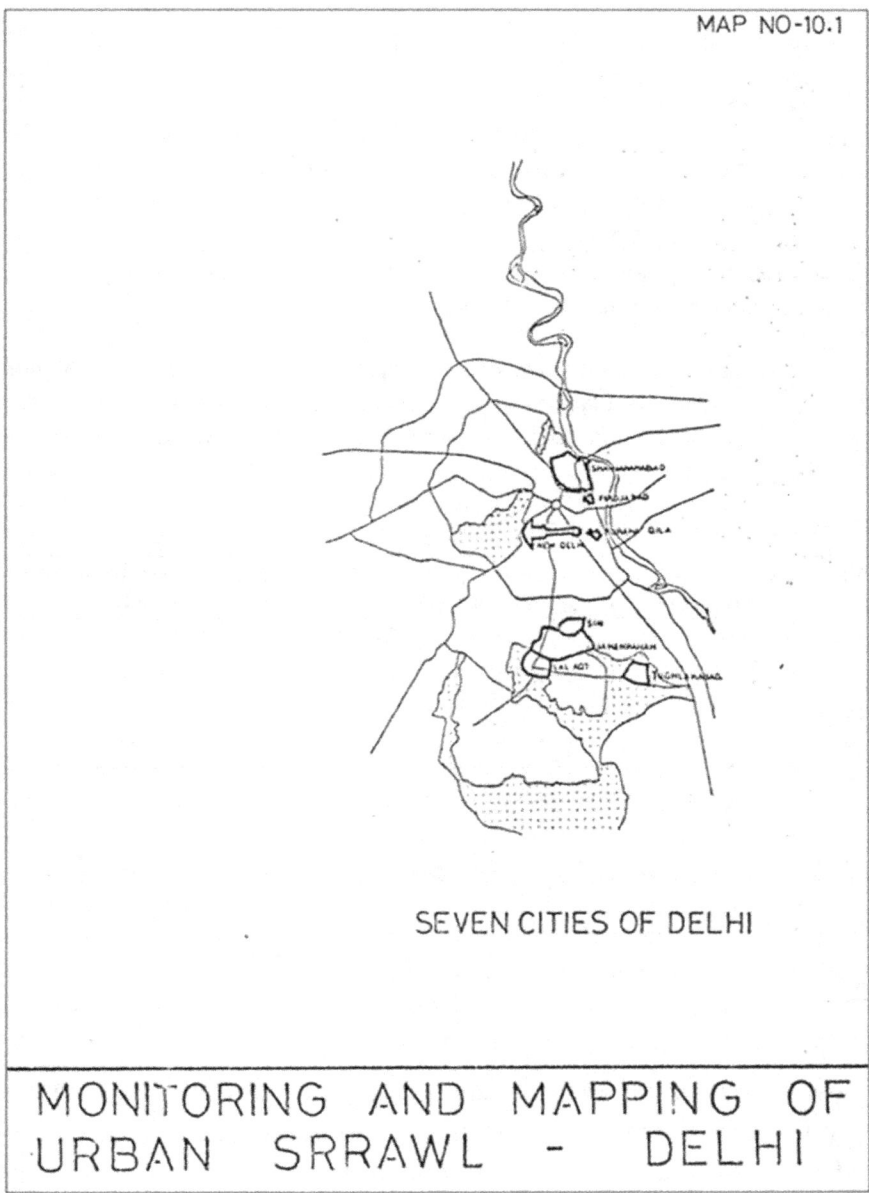

SEVEN CITIES OF DELHI

MONITORING AND MAPPING OF URBAN SRRAWL    -    DELHI

**Table 9.1** Growth of urban population in India 1901–81

| Census | Total urban population (in millions) | Percentage of urban population to total population (%) | Percentage growth of urban population during decade (%) |
|---|---|---|---|
| 1901 | 25.8 | 10.8 | – |
| 1911 | 25.9 | 10.3 | 0.3 |
| 1921 | 28.1 | 11.2 | 8.3 |
| 1931 | 33.5 | 12.0 | 19.0 |
| 1941 | 44.2 | 13.8 | 32.0 |
| 1951 | 62.4 | 17.3 | 14.4 |
| 1961 | 78.9 | 18.0 | 26.4 |
| 1971 | 101.1 | 19.9 | 38.2 |
| 1981 | 159.7* | 23.3 | 46.4 |

*Source*: Census of India 1971 and 1981
*Includes projected population for Assam for 1981

Since 1911, the growth rate of urban population has always been higher than that of total population. It is observed that gap in the growth rates of urban population and total population has been the widest during the decade 1971–81.

**Table 9.2** Growth of population in India

| Year | Total population (in millions) | Decadal growth rate (%) | Urban population (in millions) | Decadal growth rate (%) |
|---|---|---|---|---|
| 1951 | 361.09 | – | 62.44 | – |
| 1961 | 439.24 | 21.5 | 78.94 | 26.42 |
| 1971 | 548.16 | 24.8 | 109.11 | 38.22 |
| 1981 | 685.18* | 25.0 | 159.73 | 46.39 |

*Includes projected population of Assam for 1981

# 9.12 Methodology: Stages of the work

## 9.12.1 Pre-field activity

    (i) Study of the TM scene and diapositives

    (ii) Preparation of land use classification for land use mapping

    (iii) Visual interpretation of TM and MSS data

    (iv) Interpretation and delineation of land use from TM (FCC) scenes

    (v) Transfer of interpreted map to the base map

    (vi) Land use coding of the interpreted map

*Selection of polygons for sample checking and unidentified cases:* Systematic sample points were selected by super imposing grid of 6.5 × 6.5 cm. Sample points were designated on the intersection of grid lines. A total 132 points were thus identified on a 77 × 82 sq cm base map.

## 9.12.2    Field activity

(i)   Conducting of reconnaissance survey of the Delhi area

(ii)  Checking of un-identified  polygons

(iii) Division of the survey area into four parts to facilitate ground work

(iv)  Checking of sample points on the ground to assess interpretation accuracy (land use in and around the point area were considered)

(v)   Transferring sample points on 1:25,000 guide map of Delhi to facilitate the identification of sample points on ground

(vi)  Collection of data from secondary sources

(vii) Updating of land use / land cover map

## 9.12.3    Post-field activity

(i)   Finalization of the land use / land cover map after necessary correction

(ii)  Bringing finalized base map to the 1:50,000 scale using Kargl Reflecting Projector

(iii) Calculation of total study area and areas under various land uses

(iv)  For urban sprawl purpose, urban area delineation is done for years 1975, 1981 and 1985 by using MSS diapositives; and for year 1987, TM scheme is used.

(v)   Report writing and colouring of maps

(vi)  Assessing level of accuracy of interpretation

## 9.13    Land use / land cover classification for urban area and its environs

Basic land use classification of urban areas, adopted by urban planners, largely depends on the activity or actual use for which that parcel of land is being utilized. Definition of 'land use' given by many planning books is as follows 'main use or activity of that parcel of land, under question''. It is extremely difficult to anticipate activities or use of land from aerial photos or satellite imagery. Therefore, certain criteria are adopted to develop land use / land cover classification for Delhi.

(i) Land use / land cover classification should be as close as possible to the land use plan classification in content and nature, so that comparison is easy.

(ii) Classification should be uniform all over the area and common for all data products utilized.

(iii) While designing classification, user's needs should be kept in mind. It should be easier to understand and compatible to existing land use system.

(iv) Taking into consideration, the historical importance of Delhi, a special classification has been developed. Delhi has number of monuments, which are conserved by Archaeological Survey of India and local administration. For example, area under Qutab is very vast and beautifully landscaped. These green areas are easily detectable on imagery. Locations can be identified with the help of Topo maps. These historical monuments have been classified under (24) a sub-class of recreational classification.

## 9.13.1    The classification hierarchy

(1) *Built-up land*

(a) Residential – All habitable units where human activity is taking place (residences, offices, shops, schools, hospitals, etc.)

(b) Unplanned residential – Settlements grown organically and without well-laid roads, etc. This area is further classified based on density (visual perception).
   • High density
   • Medium density
   • Low density

(c) Planned residential – Areas which reflect planning in terms of well-laid road layout, regular plots, open spaces, etc. Following three categories adopted for detailing:
   • High density
   • Medium density
   • Low density

(d) Residential with tree/vegetation cover – Residential areas having tree-studded avenues and large areas under plantation. Further classification as below:
   • High density
   • Medium density
   • Low density

(e) Rural settlements –Villages and hamlets outside the settlements are considered under this category.

(f) Mixed built-up land – Areas which are under mixed type of activities are not purely under residential use.

(g) Industrial/sheds – Large industrial estates that stand out in imagery by their character and associated factors.

(h) Built-up land under construction – Land with developed infrastructure like roads etc., which layout is visible, but very few houses are constructed.

(2) *Recreation* – Areas which are interpreted as park/gardens because of their regular shape and vegetation. Detail classification is given below:

• Parks/gardens

• Play grounds/stadia

• Golf course/race course

• Special classification for historical monuments

(3) *Transportation and communication* – Land under active transportation use like roads, railways, bridges, etc. Details of classification/ sub-classes are given in Annexure below.

(4) *Vacant land* – Pockets of land within developed area which do not have any building or any vegetation cover but it has a well-defined boundary.

(5) *Agriculture land* – Cultivated land with or without crops, plantation, gardens, orchards, etc.

(6) *Forest land* – Area under naturally grown trees, vegetation. All reserved, protected forests fall under this category.

(7) *Water bodies* – All natural water bodies like lake, *nala*, river, canal, reservoirs, tanks, ponds, etc. and man-made canals are covered under this classification.

(8) *Waste land* – Land which is not suitable for cultivation or any other purpose that would benefit the community. Mostly degraded, fallow, ravine, etc., are covered under this category.

(9) *Others* – Any land use which is not covered in the previous classes is covered in this classification.

For better understanding of TM interpretation techniques and underlying assumption, a sample interpretation key is prepared (Refer Map 13.2).

INTERPRETATION KEYS -TM , DELHI SCENE 1987

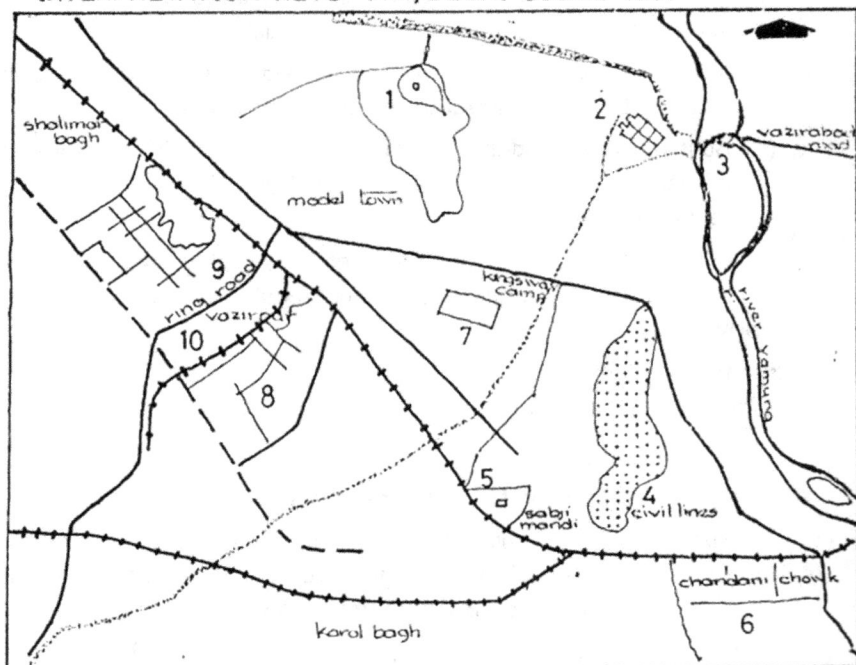

| Sr No | Code | Interpretation | Remarks |
|-------|------|----------------|---------|
| 1 | 999 | field check needed | Waterlogged area |
| 2 | 74 | shallow tanks/ponds | oxidation pond |
| 3 | 36 | bridges / culvert | Barrage cum road |
| 4 | 62 | medium forest | Ridge with greenary |
| 5 | 21 | parks / garden | Garden |
| 6 | 111 | unplan/hi. dens/res. | Walled city area |
| 7 | 212 | pl. ground / stadia. | police ground |
| 8 | 122 | med. dens/ resi. | Vazirpur colony |
| 9 | 123 | low dens./ resi. | shalimar-baug colony |
| 10 | 16 | indu. / comarcial | Vazirpur indu. area. |

Delhi: An Emerging Megacity Region

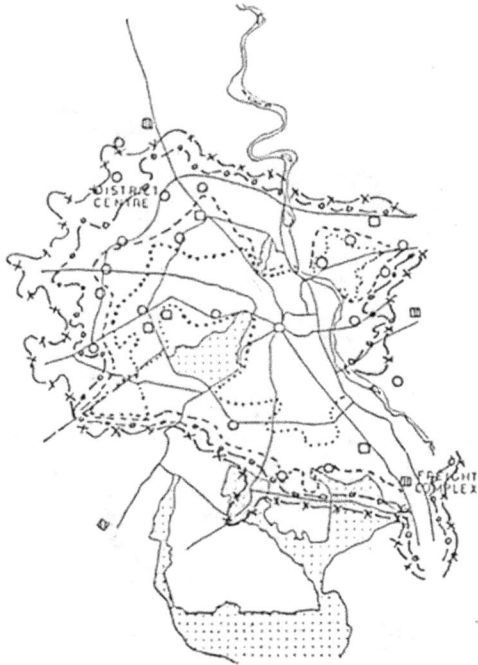

Legend:
..... UP TO 1975
- - - - 1975 - 1981
-o-•- 1981 - 1985
-x-x- 1985 - 1987

# MONITORING AND MAPPING OF URBAN SPRAWL - DELHI

Delhi: An Emerging Megacity Region

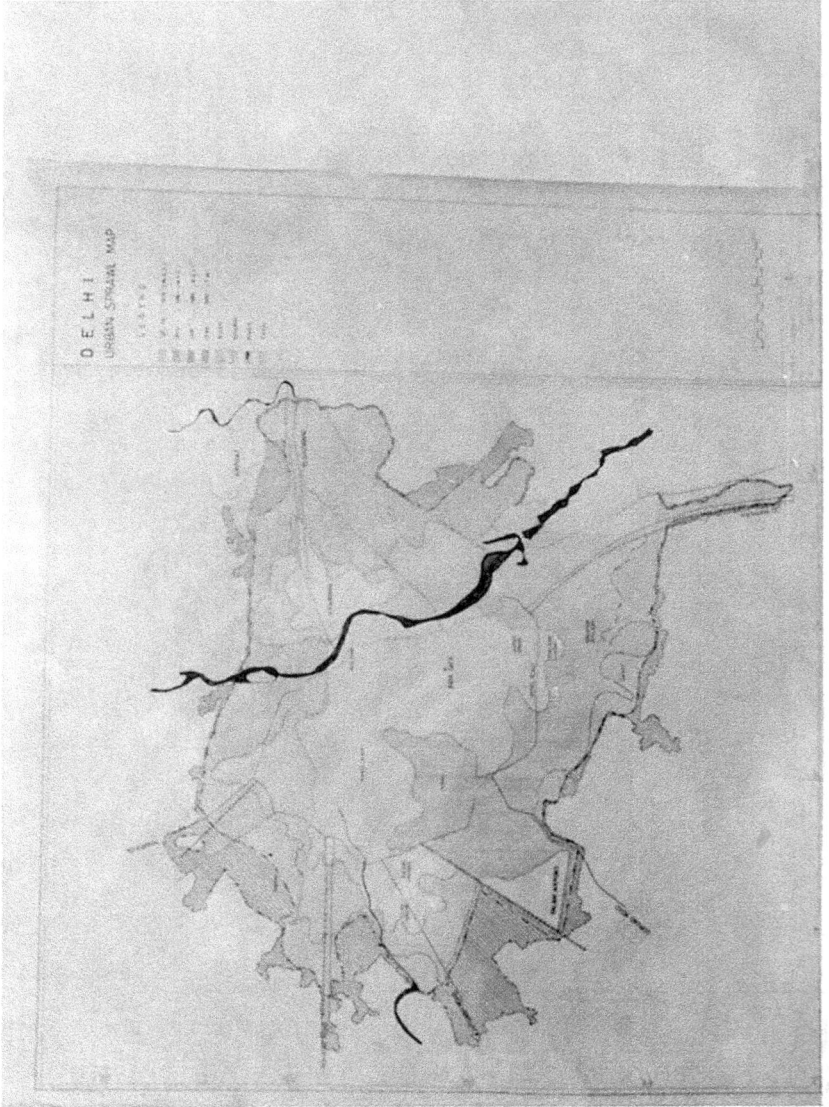

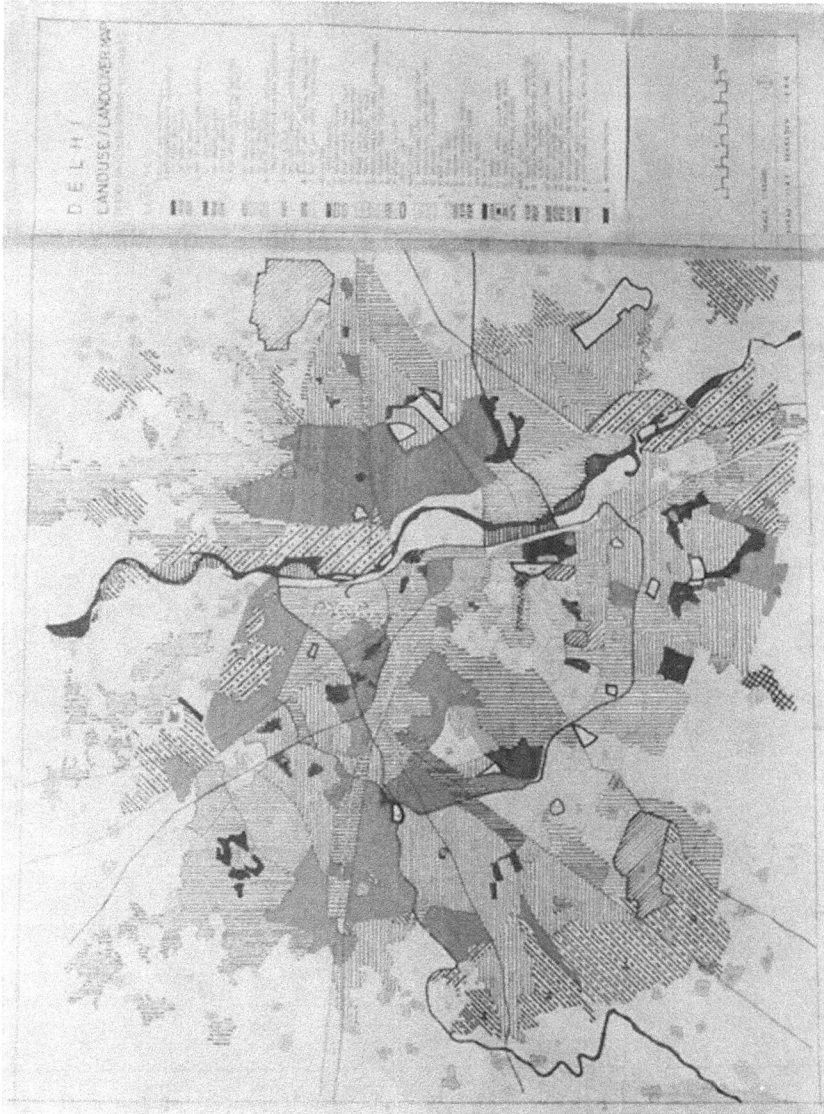

DELHI
LANDUSE / LANDCOVER '88

Monitoring and mapping of urban sprawl Delhi, 1988

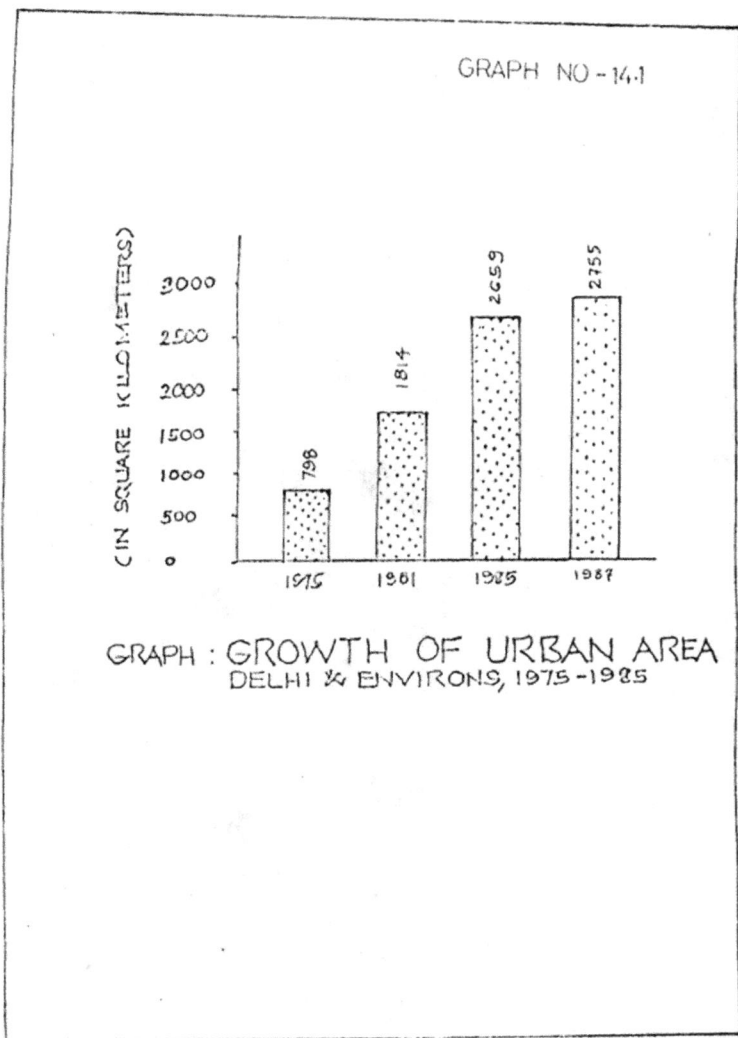

GRAPH NO - 14.1

(IN SQUARE KILOMETERS)

| Year | Value |
|------|-------|
| 1975 | 798 |
| 1981 | 1814 |
| 1985 | 2659 |
| 1987 | 2755 |

GRAPH : GROWTH OF URBAN AREA
DELHI & ENVIRONS, 1975-1985

MONITORING AND MAPPING OF URBAN SPRAWL - DELHI

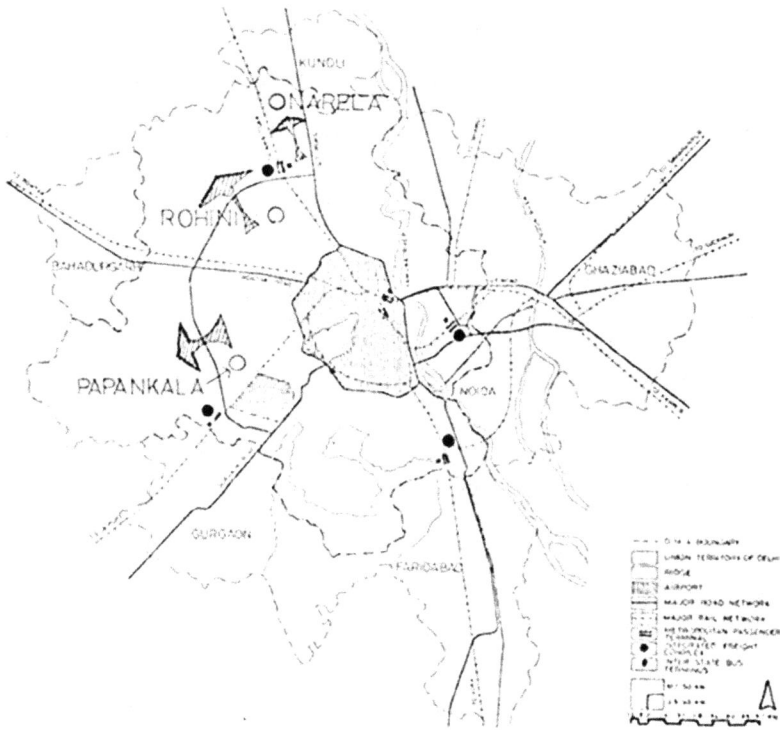

MAP NO-14.3

DELHI METROPOLITAN AREA

DIRECTION OF GROWTH

MONITORING AND MAPPING OF
URBAN SPRAWL  -   DELHI

## 9.14    Analysis

### 9.14.1    Urban sprawl

Growth of the urban agglomeration of Delhi is phenomenal. During the period 1975 and 1981, almost 1000 sq km of area was added to existing 7989 sq km of Delhi in 1975 (Fig. 14.1). The growth of Delhi's urban sprawl is as follows:

**Table 9.3** Growth of urban sprawl

| Year | Total area in (sq km) | Net addition during the period (sq km) | Growth (%) |
|------|------|------|------|
| 1975 | 798 | – | – |
| 1981 | 1814 | 1016 | 127% |
| 1985 | 2659 | 845 | 45% |
| 1987 | 2755 | 96 | 3.6% |

Growth during 1975 and 1981 period is much faster. In 1975, limit of the urban sprawl was up to Kailash Colony in South and growth was mostly confined to Shahdara town in East. In 1981, further down south, Greater Kailash was developed and on east side, beyond Yamuna, many trans-Yamuna colonies like, Mayur Vihar, Vivek Vihar were developed. Major growth took place mostly in south and east Delhi during 1975 and 1981.

After 1981, development between year 1981 and 1985 was mostly on northwest and northeast boundary of Delhi and southern limit of the city was stretched further down by development of Saket in south Delhi.

Development during 1985 and 1987 is mostly confined to the fringe areas of Delhi. Vasant Kunj residential area was developed in deep south, and fringe development took place north / north-west.

Further grown of Delhi is in north-west directions. Delhi will be expanding in this direction beyond Rohini (Fig. 9.2).

### 9.14.2    Interpretation accuracy

Once interpretation was finalized and mapped, it was tested by a method explained earlier in the methodology.

Total 132 points were marked as sample points on the map, out of these 120 points were correctly interpreted. This gives an overall accuracy rate of 89 percent, while error and omissions comprise 11 percent. Except for high density unplanned residential area classification, high level of accuracy is achieved for all other classifications (Table 9.4).

High density unplanned residential areas are generally confused with industrial or mixed use land because of similar appearance on imagery.

### 9.14.3    Areas under various land uses

Based on the interpretation, areas under various land use have been computed and given in Table 9.4.

Total area covered by this mapping was 1,30,900 hectares, out of this 69,535 is under agriculture use. Total built-up area is 61,365 hectares.

## 9.15    Conclusions and recommendations

Use of remote sensing data products for urban sprawl and land use mapping purpose has served its objective; those are mentioned in the earlier chapter. Exposure to various remotely sensed data products like MSS, TM, SPOT imagery has helped trainees to understand usefulness and limitations of these products compared to aerial photographs. Various aspects of these data products are discussed below:

- Remotely sensed data like TM covers large area and gives synoptic view. Areas where base maps are not available, these can act as substitute for the time being. It can be used for updating purpose.
- In comparison to SPOT imagery, TM and MSS have severe limitations. Spatial resolution of SPOT formed better and built areas can be clearly identified.
- TM is found suitable for the study of green areas, water bodies and natural features like ridge, hillocks, etc.
- Water bodies and water channels are easily identified on TM scene.
- Study of natural features like ridge, forest, etc., is possible from TM. In case of Delhi, central ridge which is believed to be under green area was found to be not so green and mostly rocky area.

Outer ridge extending in Haryana was easy to identify and delineate with the help of TM.

It may be concluded that:

(i)   Remote sensing data products have limited use in study of urban areas.

(ii)  Indirect application of remote sensing data products are many, like for small format aerial photography, substitute for base maps, etc.

(iii) Interpretation quality of remote sensing data products depends on the maturity and experience of the interpreter.

(iv) Remote sensing data products may be used for specific study purposes, e.g. study of vegetation or green areas, etc.

(v) Because of poor ground resolutions, remote sensing data products cannot provide wealth of information as much as aerial photographs.

## 9.16 References

1. Darin H. Brabkin – Land Policy & Urban Growth.

2. Avery, T.E and G.L. Berlin – Interpretation of Aerial Photographs, 4th ed., Burgars Minneapolis, Minn., 1985.

3. American Society of Photogrammetry, Manual of Remote Sensing, 2nd ed., Falls Church, Va, 1983.

4. Barret, E.C. and L.F. Curtis, Introduction to Environmental Remote Sensing, 2nd ed., Halsted Press, Wiley, N.Y. 1982.

5. Jensen, J.R. & D/L/ Toll – Detecting Residential Land use Development at the Urban Fringe "Photogrammetric Engineering & Remote Sensing, Vol. 48, No. 4, April 1982 pp. 629–643.

6. Lillesand, T.M. and R.W. Kiefer, Remote Sensing and Image Interpretation, 2nd ed.,

7. John Wiley & Sons.

**Table 9.4** Break-up of built-up area

| S. no. | Land use | Area (Ha) | Percentage |
|---|---|---|---|
| 1. | Residential | 33201 | 54.20% |
| 2. | Rural settlement | 2275 | 3.70% |
| 3. | Mixed built-up land | 4394 | 7.16% |
| 4. | Built-up land (industrial) | 2294 | 3.74% |
| 5. | Recreational | 2053 | 3.55% |
| 6. | Transportation & communication | 1903 | 3.10% |
| 7. | Vacant land | 834 | 1.36% |
| 8. | Forest land | 5675 | 9.25% |
| 9. | Water bodies | 1264 | 2.06% |
| 10. | Waste lands | 7472 | 12.17% |
| | Sub-total | 61,365 ha | 100.00% |
| 11. | Agriculture land | 69,535 | |
| | Grand total | 1,30,900 ha | |

**Table 9.5** Area under various land uses

| S. no. | Area (in Ha.) | Percentage | Built-up area | Sub-total |
|--------|---------------|------------|---------------|-----------|
| 111 | 5920 | 9.65 | | |
| 112 | 2375 | 3.90 | | |
| 113 | – | – | | |
| 121 | 4687 | 7.63 | | |
| 122 | 10,376 | 16.90 | | |
| 123 | 4993 | 8.13 | | |
| 131 | 397 | 0.70 | | |
| 132 | 76 | 0.12 | | |
| 133 | 4377 | 7.13 | 33201 | (54/1%) |
| 14 | 2275 | 3.70 | 2275 | (3.70) |
| 15 | 4394 | 7.16 | 4375 | (7/16) |
| 16 | 2294 | 3.73 | 2294 | (3/74) |
| 21 | 1444 | 2.35 | | |
| 22 | 136 | 0.22 | | |
| 23 | 142 | 0.23 | | |
| 24 | 331 | 0.54 | 2053 | (3.35) |
| 34 | 19 | 0.03 | | |
| 35 | 1884 | 3.07 | 1903 | (3.10) |
| 4 | 834 | 1.36 | 834 | (1.37) |
| 62 | 168 | 0.27 | | |
| 63 | 1417 | 2.30 | | |
| 64 | 4090 | 6.66 | 5675 | (9.25) |
| 71 | 989 | 1.61 | | |
| 72 | 00 | – | | |
| 73 | 216 | 0.35 | | |
| 74 | 59 | 0.10 | | |
| 83 | 587 | 0.95 | | |
| 84 | 5656 | 9.21 | | |
| 85 | 62 | 0.10 | | |
| 86 | 897 | 1.46 | | |
| 87 | 279 | 0.44 | 7472 | (12.17%) |
| Sub-total | 61,365 ha | 100.00% | 61,365 | |
| 51 | 59,127 | | | |
| 52 | 10,408 | 69,535 | | |
| Grand total | | 1,30,900 ha | | |

**Appendix 9.1** Land use / land cover classification for urban area and its surroundings

1. Built-up land
   (a) Residential
   (b) Unplanned residential
      - High density
      - Medium density
      - Low density
   (c) Planned residential
      - High density
      - Medium density
      - Low density
   (d) Residential with tree/vegetation cover
      - High density
      - Medium density
      - Low density
   (e) Rural settlement (including fringe and suburban settlements)
   (f) Mixed built-up Land (includes commercial, institutional, public and semi-public)
   (g) Industrial area/sheds
   (h) Built-up land under construction
2. Recreational
   (a) Parks/gardens
   (b) Playgrounds/stadiums
   (c) Golf course/racecourse
3. Transportation/communication
   (a) Road (metalled/major)
   (b) Roads (metalled/minor)
   (c) Roads (unmetalled/under construction)
   (d) Railway track/station/yard
   (e) Airport
   (f) Bridges/culverts

4. Vacant land

5. Agricultural land
    (a) Agriculture land (under crop)
    (b) Agricultural lands (without crop)
    (c) Orchards/plantations
6. Forest lands
    (a) Dense forests
    (b) Medium forests
    (c) Low/degraded forests
    (d) Bush/grass cover
7. Water bodies
    (a) River
    (b) Canal
    (c) Tanks/ponds (clean water)
    (d) Tanks/ponds (shallow water, turbid)
    (e) Open sewerage/drains
8. Waste lands
    (a) Gullied /ravenous land/eroded land
    (b) Undulating land, with or without forest
    (c) River sand, sandcast area
    (d) Salt affected land
    (e) Water logged areas (under water)
    (f) Backswamps
    (g) Barren/rocky areas
9. Others
    (a) Field check

# 10

# Application of GIS and Remote Sensing in planning, management and monitoring at urban fringe areas

## 10.1 Introduction

Urbanisation all over the world as a fall out of economic reforms has resulted in the concentration of population around metropolitan cities and rapid expansion of urban limits. Gradual absorption of rural areas within metropolitan limits and pressure on agriculture land is a major problem in urban fringe areas. Urban fringe area of any city is a dynamic entity where land use transformation is very fast. In contrast, process of planning and land use allocation is very slow, which may result in contradiction between planning proposals and ground reality. Therefore mapping and updating of base maps for an urban fringe area is a major challenge. Another major task is to monitor frequent changes taking place in urban fringe areas of the city.

## 10.2 GIS and Remote Sensing techniques

At this juncture GIS and Remote Sensing technologies have emerged as an important instrument/tool for mapping and monitoring of land component. The land related technologies are very useful in collection of data related to land, terrain and environment.

Satellite imageries substitute for aerial photographs and base maps as both are difficult to get at regular intervals due to following reasons:

(a) Planning, execution and delivery in both the cases take years. By the time data are made available, it is already obsolete due to time lag.

(b) Security clearance which is mandatory takes considerable time.

(c) Cost and logistic involved in both the cases are exorbitant.

### 10.2.1 Location

Use of satellite imageries in Rohini Project of Delhi Development Authority (DDA) was found very useful. This project or sub-city for 1 million population spread over 5000 ha of land is located in the North West of Delhi (Fig. 10.1). Existing base maps were at least 10 years old or in some cases simply not available.

**Figure 10.1** Location plan of Delhi

## 10.2.2 Instruments used

First time in 1996, satellite imageries of IRS–IC were made available for urban application by National Remote Sensing Agency (NRSA), Department of Space, Government of India. DDA utilized panchromatic encoded satellite imageries at the scale of 1:12,500 for updating of base maps and monitoring change detection within the urban fringe area of Rohini Project. It also provided valuable inputs for urban planning.

## 10.3 Interpretation of satellite imageries

Image interpretation is defined as an act of examining images to identify objects and convert interpreted data into information/overlay/map. This is an important task as it leads to classification of land uses or land cover for area under interpretation.Any satellite imagery is capable of detecting linear features like major roads, drains, river /nallah, railway lines, settlements/ villages, land under cultivation / without cultivation, etc.

However, quality of interpretation depends on ground resolution (minimum detectable size of an object on ground) of the satellite imageries and experience of the interpreter. However, in some cases an experienced interpreter may be able to identify revenue boundaries of villages on satellite imagery as agriculture field / cultivated land tend to change its shape and size along the revenue boundary of that field. Thus it can be easily correlated with revenue boundary of villages on khasra map / cadastre map.This is possible because revenue holdings are regular in shape and equal in size in the northern part of Delhi where Rohini Project is situated.

## 10.4 Change detection

Remote sensing is used for land use change detection by comparing satellite imageries of two different dates. It has been observed that in urban fringe areas major change has occurred in the conversion of cultivated land into non-cultivated land. Such change in status of land is clearly visible on the satellite imagery.

The detection of such change is extremely useful from land management point of view. It could be the beginning of encroachment or unauthorized settlement.Thus identified areas on satellite imagery could be notified to field staff for site checking.

## 10.5 Monitoring

One of the major problems faced by any land-owning agency like DDA is protection of its acquired land as planning and development of such land takes considerable time. It has been experienced that large scale conversion of agriculture land into non-agricultural land can be easily detected from satellite imageries. For monitoring of land acquired by DDA, satellite imageries of the month of February,April and November 1996 were utilized. Changes detection in land cover/ vegetation cover interpreted and transferred on a map of 1:10,000 scale (Figs. 10.2 and 10.3).

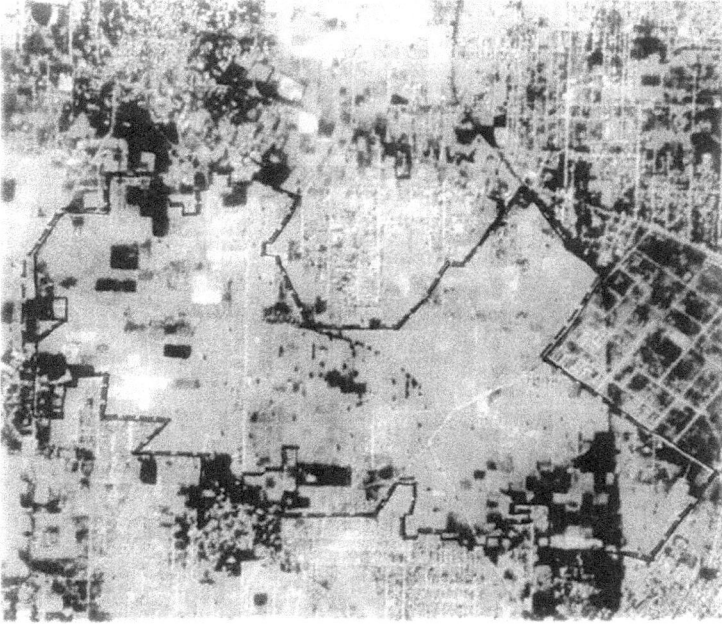

**Figure 10.2** Change detection and seasonal variation (November, 1996)

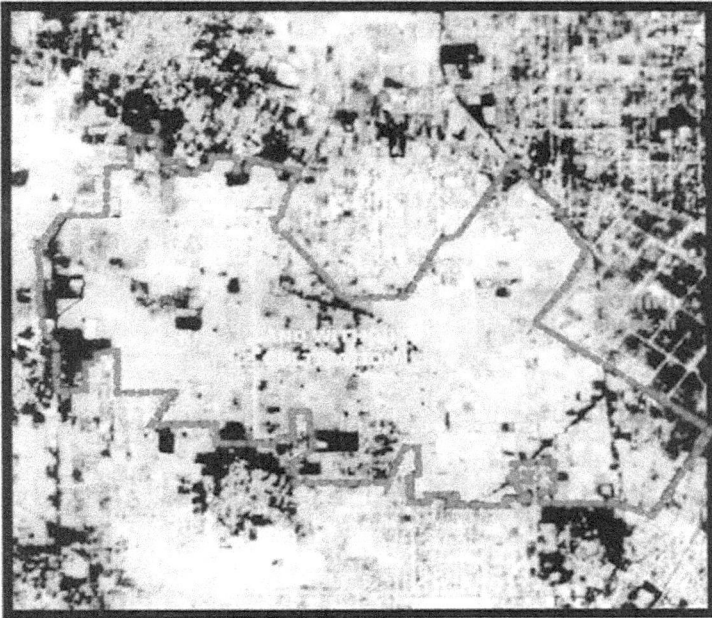

**Figure 10.3** Change detection and seasonal variation in Rohini and surrounding area

## 10.6　Detection of vacant land

For land acquisition purposes, it is important to have record of status of land, i.e. whether it is a vacant land or built-up land on the day authorities decide to acquire land. Such information may also prove to be useful for deciding legal/compensation cases. In case of Rohini, it was observed from satellite imageries that a large chunk of land is lying vacant adjacent to the existing sector nos. 20, 21 and 22 of Rohini Phase-III. It was found that acquisition of such land would be beneficial to DDA as it is continuous to the already developed area by DDA. Acquisition of this type of land may result in cost saving in terms of cost of development of land and infrastructure. This pocket of vacant land was not visible on ground as it was surrounded by built-up areas (Fig. 10.4).

**Figure 10.4**　Vacant pockets detected from satellite imagery of Rohini

## 10.7　Conclusion

Technologies like GIS and Remote Sensing help to rationalize decision-making process of planners as well as administrators, especially when it comes to crucial decisions related to land acquisition, removal of encroachment and implementation of time-bound projects. For planning purposes, satellite imageries provide an overview of the area, profile of the terrain and a reasonable idea about its natural surroundings. Satellite imageries are useful in urban planning for the following reasons:

- Updating of base maps which are old.
- Identifying or co-relating the revenue boundaries of villages based on ground features as identified on the satellite imageries.
- Identification of vacant land for acquisition, planning and development.
- Monitoring of land change detection.
- Locating alignment of major roads, railway and H.T. lines.
- Implementing projects and demarking layouts.

Remote sensing has the capability to provide Fourth Dimension (time) and Sense of History as it maintains faithful record of the past.

# Index

## A
Aibak, Qutub-ud-din, 99

## B
Built heritage, 23

## C
Capacity building, 29
Capitals, 28
City dwellers, 16
Clusters of monuments, 28–29
Conservation plan, 29
Conservation zone, plan for, 27–29
    heritage components, spatial
    extent, 27
    qualities to be preserved,
    27–28
    zones, delineation of, 28
Cultural entity or culture region,
    25
Cultural landscapes, 26

## D
Delhi
    Civil Lines, 100
    evolution of, 98–100
    seven cities of, 98–100
    water supply, existing scenario
    of, 82–83
Delhi Jal Board (DJB), 83

Delhi Metropolitan Area (DMA), 95
Delhi, decongestion of
    decentralized infrastructure
    systems, need for, 13
    demarcation of influence zone
    in zonal plans, 12
    Ministry of Urban
    Development
    recommendations, 12–14
    Parking management district
    plans, need for, 13
Delhi Development Authority
    master plan in 1991 (MPD
    2001), 16–17, 17f
    compulsory large-scale land
    acquisition, 18
    implementation of the
    proposals, uncertainties of
    changing environment, 17
    non-access to affordable
    housing of public sector, 18
    strict land use zoning, 18
Delhi, master plan, policies
    monitoring and
    implementation, 65–68
    projects and policies, 69–71
    proposals of MPD 2001 and
    implementation in urban
    extension, 65t–68t
    structure plan, 65
Delhi, unauthorized colonies, 18–19
Delhi, water management, 85–89

declining water level, 87–88

ground water table, management of, 86–89

rain water harvesting, Central Groundwater Board of NCT Delhi, 88

water resources & water treatment, 86

Delhi, water supply problems, 83–85

areas lacking adequate focus, 85

disparity in supply, 84

inter-agency co-ordination, lack of, 84

local groundwater and its non-management, 85

over dependence on planned funds, 85

sources outside Delhi, dependence on, 84–85

unaccounted for water, 84

Delhi's heritage, 24–25

ASI, agency for protection of heritage, 24–25

Dillu–Dilli–Delhi, 98

Dinpanah, 99

Dwarka

population norms and space standards, 69

**G**

Gallon per capita per day (GPCD), 82

Germany, spatial environmental planning, 51–63

as a "bottom–up process", 56

as a "conflict coordination theatre", 55

decentralised execution power, 54

effectiveness, 53–54

environmental consideration, planning concepts, 52

environmental criteria, 59

Environmental Impact Analysis (EIA), 52

environmental objectives, 52, 56–57

German environmental administration, 52

industrial estates, planning and implementation of, 59–61

industrial planning estates, 60

mitigation planning, 60

public participation, 61–62

soft planning tools, 56

standards versus procedures, 55–56

urban renewal programs, 61–62

water protection zone, 57–58

water quality management objectives, 58–59

GIS, 118

**H**

Heritage zones, 26

Historic villages, 28

**I**

India

independence of, impact on towns and cities, 72

land use planning and master plan, driving policies and procedures of, 42

master plan, past experience,
16–19
urban planning, challenges, 16
urbanization, 100–102
urbanization challenges, 15
Indraprastha, 98
Influence zone plans (IZP), 13

**J**

Jahanpanah, 99

**K**

Karkardooma pilot project, 5
Karkardooma smart city hub, 5
Karkardooma TOD project, 5–12
access and connectivity to the
site, 5
concept adopted, 9–10
decentralized infrastructure, 14
design option, scenario
explored, 5–7
housing delivery, 11–12
informal colonies in
surrounding areas, 9
MRTS corridors as per MPD
2021, 5
planned colonies in
surrounding areas, 8–9
preliminary traffic impact
assessment, 5
stakeholder consultations, 8
TOD integrated schemes, 12
TOD norms, 12

**L**

Land use, 91
definition, 103

**M**

Master plan, 16
proposals, 18
Master Plan 2021 (MPD 2021)
archaeological park, 30
areas identified as heritage
zones, 32f
conservation strategy, 29–30
cultural resource management
plan, 37f
entrance areas… forecourt to
Qutub complex, 39f
heritage sites, environmental
degradation issues, 36
heritage trail… Intach in
collaboration with DTTDC,
37f–38f
Heritage zone, 30
Mehrauli… historic background,
33f
redefining missing links,
39f–41f
scope of heritage, 31
site potentials… historic
structures, 35f
site potentials… physiography
and hydrology, 34f
site potentials… vegetation, 35f
special conservation plans,
30–31
Master Plan for Delhi 1962, 24
Master Plan for Delhi 2001, 24
Master plan for Delhi 2021 (MPD
2021), 20–21
cutoff date for regularization,
46
future policy formulation, land

policy for, 20

local area plan (LAP), 21

regularization after the notification, steps to follow, 46

regularization of unauthorized colonies, procedure for, 45–50

unauthorized colonies, regularization of, 21

Master Plan for Delhi, 1981–2001, 64

Master Plan for Delhi, perspective 2001

    monitoring, built-in provision for, 92

Master plan, procedure-based planning, 43–44

    bottom–up procedures, 44

    current land use planning practice, 43

MPD-2001

    development code and monitoring, 69

    population norms and space standards, 69

    population projections of, 69

MPD 2021

    provisions for, 20–21

MPD 2021, conceptual framework on heritage conservation, 25–27

    conservation management plan, 26

    general policies, 26–27

    information management, 26

    informed decision-making, 26

MPD 2021, critical areas

    land assembly, procedure for, 45

    procedure-based planning, 44–45

MPD 2021, procedure-based planning initiated, 45

    local area plan, 45

    unauthorized colonies, regularization of, 45

MPD 2021, regularization of unauthorized colonies, procedure for, 42–50

    Clause 8(2), public and semi-public facilities in residential and other use zones, 49

    cut-off date for regularization, 46

    extent of buildable area, 49

    mixed use, 48–49

    regularization after the notification, steps to follow, 46–47

    Section 57 of DD Act on 24 March 2008, 45–46

    special area and villages, 47

    special area plans, 47

    spot zoning, 49–50

    villages, plans for, 47–48

## P

Planners

    need to understand political urgency, 78

Procedure-based planning

    bottom-up procedures, 19, 43–44

    controlled development of land, top–down approach of, 42

for critical areas, 20, 44
fundamentals of, 19–20
initiated in MPD 2021, 21
land use planning, 19–20, 71
master plan preparation, 20
MPD-2001 proposals, 43
people-oriented procedures
and trust-based planning
system, 27–28
urban planning, past experience, 43
Purani Delhi, 99–100

## R

Remote sensing, 92–93
technologies, 118–119

## S

Sanitation facility, 83
Satellite imageries, 118
instruments used, 119
interpretation of, 119–120
land use change detection, 120
location, 118
monitoring, 120–121
Siri, 98–99
Structure plan, 16
Surajkund, 98

## T

TOD planning, 1
TOD policy, 1
Master Plan for Delhi 2021,
1–2
TOD retrofitting, 1
TOD zone
goal of, 2

green buildings, 3
green public open space provision,
3
impact assessment, 3
mix of uses, 4
planning and design
parameters, 2–3
social infrastructure, 3
Town planning, 64, 72–73
end of 19th century and the
first half of 20th century, 73
from fifties to the seventies, 74
last quarter of twentieth
century, 74
twenty first century, 75
Traditional planning, 16
Transit Oriented Development
(TOD), 1
Tughlaq, Firoz Shah, 99
Tughlaqabad, 26, 99

## U

Urban area, land use / land cover
classification, 103–111
built-up land, 104–105
classification hierarchy, 104–
111
criteria for Delhi, 104–111
Urban fringe area, 118
Urban growth, 80, 93
important phenomena
associated, 91
Urban planners
land use plan, objective of,
93–94
Urban planning process
monitoring, 92

**129**

Urban planning
Delhi Master Plan 2021 Guidelines, 76–77
  DoE circular 22/80, 75
  emerging trends in, 76–78
  Green Paper, 75–76
Master Plan for Delhi 2021, innovative features, 77–78
  master plans, limitations of, 76
  master plans, morphology of, 72–75
  past trends, 75–76
  physical planning, operational area, 72
Urban population
  provision for water, challenges for, 80–82
Urban sprawl Delhi, 1988,

monitoring and mapping, 91–117
  analysis, 112–113
  interpretation accuracy, 112–113
objectives, 93–94
  remote sensing, 92–93
Urban villages, 29

**V**

Vacant land, detection of, 122

**W**

Water usage
  ancient times, 1
  challenges related to, 80
  historical times, 81–82